FORMATIVE ASSESSMENT

For Philippa
1959–2009

FORMATIVE ASSESSMENT

Making
It
Happen
in the
Classroom

MARGARET HERITAGE

Foreword by James W. Stigler

CORWIN
A SAGE Company

For information:

Corwin
A SAGE Company
2455 Teller Road
Thousand Oaks, California 91320
(800) 233-9936
Fax: (800) 417-2466
www.corwin.com

SAGE India Pvt. Ltd.
B 1/I 1 Mohan Cooperative
   Industrial Area
Mathura Road, New Delhi 110 044
India

SAGE Ltd.
1 Oliver's Yard
55 City Road
London EC1Y 1SP
United Kingdom

SAGE Asia-Pacific Pte. Ltd.
33 Pekin Street #02-01
Far East Square
Singapore 048763

Printed in the United States of America

Library of Congress Cataloging-in-Publication Data

Heritage, H. Margaret.
Formative assessment : making it happen in the classroom / H. Margaret Heritage.
      p. cm.
Includes bibliographical references and index.
ISBN 978-1-4129-7504-9 (pbk.)
   1. Educational tests and measurements. 2. Effective teaching. I. Title.

LB3051.H445 2010
371.26'4—dc22   2010001673

This book is printed on acid-free paper.

10   11   12   13   14   10   9   8   7   6   5   4   3   2   1

Acquisitions Editor:	Cathy Hernandez
Associate Editor:	Desirée A. Bartlett
Editorial Assistant:	Kimberly Greenberg
Production Editor:	Eric Garner
Copy Editor:	Terri Lee Paulsen
Typesetter:	C&M Digitals (P) Ltd.
Proofreader:	Joyce Li
Indexer:	Judy Hunt
Cover Designer:	Michael Dubowe

Contents

Foreword

James W. Stigler

Teaching itself may not have changed much over the past several decades. But how we *think* about teaching—what the job entails, and its importance—is changing rapidly. With all the current discussions of standards and testing, it is sometimes easy to forget that the standards movement in U.S. education has only existed for a brief time. Not that long ago, teachers felt they had great latitude to choose what they wanted to teach. Many thought that "good teaching" was defined by what teachers did, not necessarily by what their students were learning. And the prevailing wisdom, in any case, was that teaching itself had a relatively small impact on students' learning, dwarfed in its effect by other factors. Teachers did things, and students learned things, but few believed the learning to be caused primarily by the teaching.

All that has changed. Researchers and policy makers now see teaching as one of the most important factors affecting students' learning, and certainly the most important one over which we have any control. New approaches to judging teacher quality pay serious attention to data that indicate what students are learning. Teachers themselves are increasingly held accountable for student outcomes. Good teaching is not defined by what teachers do as much as by what students learn as a consequence. Teachers are in the forefront of education reform efforts because they are seen as the key to helping all students learn: Because teachers are there, in the classrooms, they are presumed to be the only ones with the information, knowledge, skills, and judgment to help students learn what they need to learn.

But there is one small glitch: How are teachers supposed to actually improve student learning? What tools and support do they have available to help them meet these new responsibilities? This book by Margaret Heritage is directly aimed at these questions. In highly practical terms, she gives teachers (and others engaged in the education enterprise) a nuts-and-bolts introduction to teaching as a goal-directed activity. She demonstrates the importance of clear and explicit learning goals, and then shows how to create them. Drawing on her research and that of others, Margaret Heritage introduces the critical concept of "learning progressions." If teachers are to be held accountable for specific learning outcomes, a new science is needed to determine the most effective waypoints and pathways students can pass through in order to achieve these goals. But this science does not yet exist, and so teachers must invent these learning progressions themselves, working together to figure out how to get students from where they are now to where they need to go. Margaret shows them how to do this.

Once goals are clearly defined, the next step is to create formative assessments to chart students' progress, and to guide the teachers' actions as they work to support students' learning. This is the core of the book. Margaret presents the most current research on assessment, and especially on formative assessment, in a clear and readable style. But again, the real value of this book is that she tells you *how* to do it, drawing on her years of experience as a teacher, school inspector, principal, and researcher. Formative assessment is one of the most powerful tools teachers can have in their repertoire, provided they know how to use it. Perhaps one day we will have a readily accessible knowledge base of research-tested assessments to meet every learning goal. But for now, teachers and administrators will have to take the lead. This book shows them how to go about it.

The traditional separation of research, practice, and the design and development communities has not served education well. Research that is divorced from practice does not result in usable knowledge. Practice that is not informed by research is no longer adequate in a world where educators are held accountable for outcomes. Educational tools and materials designed to sell, but not constrained by usability requirements or evidence of effectiveness, are not worth the money we spend on them. Education in the future will require an integration of research, design, and practice. Margaret Heritage provides a great example of what this new integration will look like. She offers us the best of research, of design, and of practitioners' experience, all focused on improving learning for all students.

Acknowledgments

First and foremost, I want to thank all the teachers I have worked with over many years in England and the United States who have helped me learn about formative assessment and what it means to successfully implement formative assessment in their classrooms. In particular, I have a special word of thanks for the teachers from Syracuse City School District, New York, from across Iowa, and from Para Los Niños Charter School in Los Angeles whose work you see represented in this book, and for Caroline Wylie, my coauthor for Chapter 8.

Next, I want to thank the colleagues who have supported and encouraged me and from whom I have learned much about formative assessment: Jim Popham, Joan Herman, Ellen Osmundson, Alison Bailey, Ron Gallimore, and Jim Stigler. I also thank my colleagues who assisted me with the preparation of the manuscript, Didiana Ramirez, Beth White, and Sarah Kolterman.

At Corwin, my thanks go to Cathy Hernandez for her thoughtful editorial comments and for providing me with anonymous reviews of the draft manuscript. The book is certainly a better one for their contributions.

Finally, my family and friends are gratefully acknowledged for their continued support: Philippa and Ken for their encouragement in writing the book during the summer of 2009 in Lucca, Italy, and to my husband, John, for his confidence in me and for teaching me so much about writing.

PUBLISHER'S ACKNOWLEDGMENTS

Corwin gratefully acknowledges the contributions of the following individuals:

Carol Amos, Teacher Leader and Mathematics Coordinator
Twinfield Union School
Plainfield, Vermont

Margaret Couture, Elementary Principal
South Seneca Central School District
Interlaken, New York

Diana Coyl, Associate Professor of Child Development
California State University, Chico
Chico, California

Susan D'Angelo, Fifth-Grade Gifted Education Teacher
Pineview School for the Gifted
Osprey, Florida

Nancy Gerzon, Senior Program Associate/Educational Consultant
Learning Innovations at WestEd
Woburn, Massachusetts

Sara Johnson, Director of Human Resources
Lincoln County School District
Newport, Oregon

Karen Kersey, Second-Grade Teacher
Alban Elementary
St. Albans, West Virginia

Melissa Miller, Sixth-Grade Science Instructor
Lynch Middle School
Farmington, Arkansas

Debra S. Morris, Assistant Superintendent of Curriculum & Instruction
Kannapolis City Schools
Kannapolis, North Carolina

Patti Palmer, Sixth-Grade Teacher
Wynford Schools
Bucyrus, Ohio

Jill Shackelford, Superintendent
Kansas City Public Schools
Kansas City, Kansas

Linda Taylor, Assistant Professor of Elementary Education
Ball State University
Muncie, Indiana

About the Author

 **Margaret Heritage** is Assistant Director for Professional Development at the National Center for Research on Evaluation, Standards, & Student Testing (CRESST) at the University of California, Los Angeles (UCLA) and leads the data use program of the Assessment and Accountability Comprehensive Center.

Prior to joining CRESST, she had many years of teaching and leadership experience in schools in the United Kingdom and the United States, including a period as a county inspector of education in the United Kingdom and as principal at the UCLA laboratory school. She has also taught graduate classes in education at the Department of Education at the University of Warwick, England; the University of California, Los Angeles; and at Stanford University.

Her current work focuses on data use for school improvement, learning progressions, formative assessment, and teachers' use of formative assessment evidence.

Margaret Heritage is the coauthor (with Alison Bailey) of *Formative Assessment for Literacy, Grades K–6: Building Reading and Academic Language Skills Across the Curriculum,* published by Corwin.

About the Contributor

E. Caroline Wylie is a research scientist in the Learning and Teaching Research Center at Educational Testing Service (ETS). Her current research centers on issues of teaching quality and the use of formative assessment to improve classroom teaching and learning. She is involved in projects that are focused on the creation of effective, scalable, and sustainable teacher professional development. Related research projects have focused on the formative use of diagnostic questions for classroom-based assessment and the impact that the sustained use of such questions have on classroom instruction and student learning.

Previous work at ETS includes serving as the lead ETS developer of the National Board for Professional Teaching Standards (NBPTS) certificates for middle and high school science teachers and elementary school art teachers. She also was involved in the implementation of NBPTS scoring and in designing materials for lead trainers, along with research related to issues of scoring quality.

She holds a postgraduate certificate in teaching mathematics and information technology and a doctorate in educational assessment, both from Queen's University Belfast, Northern Ireland. She has been working in the United States for the past 12 years.

Introduction

This book is about the everyday work of teachers in classrooms. It is intended for teachers and for those who support the work of teachers, and it is about making formative assessment practice an integral part of the classroom, any classroom—elementary, middle, or high school—and in any subject area: the arts, social studies, math, language arts, science, physical education, design and technology, and so on. The book is also intended for all teachers, regardless of their stage of implementing formative assessment. Those teachers who are just beginning to think about formative assessment— why do it and what it looks like in practice—will be able to use the book as a starting point, while those who are further along in implementing formative assessment in their classrooms can use it to refine and develop their knowledge and skills further.

BRIDGING THEORY, RESEARCH, AND PRACTICE

For some readers of this book, the idea of formative assessment will require a paradigm shift. For those who think effective teaching is all about a stand-and-deliver approach, where teachers lecture to students to "give" them the knowledge they need and then test them to make sure they have "got it," then the contents of this book will represent a considerable shift in thinking about how to do business in the classroom. For others, it will be a less dramatic change. Whatever perspective readers bring, bear in mind that this book is about research into practice, not just a collection of "cool" ideas about teaching and learning.

The book builds bridges between the theory and research about formative assessment and its actual practice in the classroom. The theoretical and research base is wide and deep. It ranges from Paul Black and Dylan Wiliam's now famous 1998 review of studies of formative assessment, to literature on the effects of feedback on learning, to the role that assessment can play in motivation and self-regulation. The book translates this theory and research into actual classroom practice. For the most part, the practices described are those of current teachers with varying levels of experience and who are at various stages of implementation. The examples of practice from these teachers are not intended as "counsels of perfection," but rather as examples readers can reflect on and learn from as they think about formative assessment in the classroom.

Any and all of the teachers represented in this book would say they are committed to formative assessment as a way to improve teaching and learning. They would also say they recognize assessment and the teaching process as inseparable; one cannot happen without the other. They would most likely comment that the skillful use of formative assessment is not something acquired overnight. Instead, it is a long process of learning, trying things out, and reviewing and refining—in short, of continuously engaging in a process of reflective practice. These teachers would also say that they are willing to change what they do, willing to take risks and make mistakes they can learn from, and willing to learn with, and from, their colleagues.

OVERVIEW OF THE CHAPTERS

Chapter 2 introduces formative assessment as a process and describes the elements of the process that are the focus of subsequent chapters. It is a process of formative assessment that is applicable to all classrooms in all subject areas. The theoretical and research base underpinning each element is described in terms of the contribution that each one makes to improved student learning.

Chapter 3 takes the broad view and focuses on where formative assessment fits within the big assessment picture. The chapter addresses a range of assessment sources available to teachers, all of which have a particular purpose and can be used in different ways to support curriculum planning, teaching, and learning. It locates formative assessment as the assessment closest to daily teaching and learning in classrooms.

In Chapter 4, the focus is on learning progressions, learning goals, and criteria for success. Learning goals and success criteria drive the entire formative assessment process and need to be clearly articulated by teachers and clearly understood by students. The chapter draws from a paper on learning progressions by Heritage (2007) and stresses the importance of having clear conceptions of learning in place from which teachers can identify learning goals and success criteria. The central message of the chapter is the importance of identifying the learning goal first (rather than the activities, which teachers may be tempted to do) from the learning progression, and then specifying the criteria for success. Selecting formative assessment strategies to match the goals and criteria can only be done when the goals and criteria are clearly identified.

Chapter 5 deals with selecting formative assessment strategies, interpreting evidence from formative assessment, and how the interpretation of evidence leads to instructional action. In a seminal paper in 1989, D. Royce Sadler established the essential purpose of formative assessment as the means to identify the "gap" between a learner's current status in learning and some desired educational goal. This chapter shows how teachers can use formative assessment strategies to close the gap and keep learning moving forward. The chapter also treats the evidence that teachers get from formative assessment as feedback for teaching, that is, feedback they can use to feed forward into instructional planning.

In their review of studies of formative assessment, Black and Wiliam (1998b) concluded that when formative assessment is combined with quality feedback, improvements in learning occur. Chapter 6 considers the feedback that students receive externally from their teachers and peers, and internally through their own self-monitoring during the course of learning. The chapter describes the contribution of external feedback to learning, what kind of feedback is effective and what is not, and provides plenty of examples of feedback. The chapter also considers the effects of self-assessment on learning and the skills students need to successfully engage in this activity.

Implementing formative assessment requires teachers to have specific knowledge and skills, and Chapter 7 focuses on what these are. It begins with a discussion of the kind of classroom culture teachers need to establish for formative assessment, and then details the knowledge and skills needed for formative assessment. Among the knowledge is content knowledge, pedagogical content knowledge, and knowledge of what psychologists call metacognition. The diverse range of skills teachers need include interpreting evidence, matching instruction to the learning needs to close the gap, and skills in providing feedback to students that move learning forward. In addition to specifying the requisite skills and knowledge, the chapter also offers suggestions about how they can be developed.

Teachers cannot develop the skillful use of formative assessment on their own. They need the help of colleagues and administrators. The final chapter of the book, coauthored with Caroline Wylie from the Educational Testing Service, builds on Chapter 7 by examining specific structures and practices that can be established within a school to help teachers develop and deepen formative assessment in their classroom. The chapter also addresses the kind of leadership that administrators need to provide, and that teachers should expect, to ensure they have the necessary support to engage in the work.

CHANGES IN PRACTICE

As already noted, for many teachers implementing the process of formative assessment in their classrooms will require some change in how the business of teaching and learning is conducted. For some, the change will be significant; for others less so—but some change will happen, for sure. This book is about and for teachers who engage in reflection and ongoing professional learning to make changes in what they do to benefit their students. We end this introductory chapter with some of those teachers' voices, specifically the voices of teachers from Syracuse City School District in New York, who have been working intensively for the past two years to become skillful users of formative assessment in their classrooms. Here they reflect on their journey:

Erin: Formative assessment makes my teaching much more efficient. I'm not teaching the unit for two months because they're still not getting it! Some units we've taught in the past that we've talked about today took us *weeks* and *weeks* to teach. Now they're taking us two weeks and everyone's getting it! . . . Our whole room is improving. We still have kids who are struggling, but they've made progress on that learning progression.

Maryanne: Formative assessment is not more work, it's better work.

Sharon: I used to do more, but now I do less. Because so much evidence is gathered with formative assessment, I may do two or three very targeted tasks in an 80-minute class rather than "lots of good stuff." Now I work hard to save time for student reflection rather than filling every minute with activity. I take every opportunity to assess my students in various, formative ways. I'm not asking them for three of four different pieces of paper at the end of class so I can tell them if they "got it." Now, they may only produce one piece of written evidence in their learning; I have other ways of assessing them now that can inform me of where they are throughout the lesson. I can address misconceptions more quickly and push their learning farther with timely feedback.

Shawn: I used to do a lot of *explaining,* but now I do a lot of *questioning.* I used to do *a lot of talking,* but now I do *a lot of listening.* I use to think *about teaching the curriculum,* but now I think *about teaching the student.*

(Shawn's emphases)

Melanie: I used to think that formative assessment was just the assessment teachers use to figure out if students understood the lesson or not, but I now think that formative assessment is a process which is a series of planning, reflection, and feedback by the teacher and the student. This process seems to be something I have been missing from my own teaching.

Sharon: I feel like formative assessment has helped me enter into a partnership with students with regard to learning. It has helped me demystify the classroom for kids. The transparency that sharing learning goals and success criteria creates allows for so much growth for both teacher and student. The students know I am there because I have a goal for them to reach and I want them to succeed. They also know I take every opportunity (written work, conversations, response boards . . .) to gather evidence of what they know. Formative assessment has not only changed me as a teacher, but I believe it has changed the students as learners.

Enjoy the journey!

2 Assessment With and for Students

The word "assessment" comes from the Latin verb "assidere," meaning "to sit with." This word origin implies that in assessment the teacher sits with the learner and assessment is something teachers do *with* and *for* students rather than *to* students (Green, 1998).

Formative assessment, in particular, is something teachers do *with* and *for* students. Teachers involve students *with* them in the assessment, thus students and teachers are partners, both sharing responsibility for learning. Formative assessment provides evidence *for* improving student learning. Indeed, to emphasize this function, it is often referred to as "assessment *for* learning." Lorna Earl (2003) also uses the phrase "assessment as learning," signaling the active role students play in the process.

A major landmark in the emergence of formative assessment was a synthesis of research findings from conducted by Paul Black and Dylan Wiliam in 1998. This review, and the more commonly read *Phi Delta Kappan* article in the same year, led to the widespread recognition of formative assessment as a powerful method for improving all students' learning. They concluded that student learning gains triggered by formative assessment were "amongst the largest ever reported for educational interventions," with the largest gains being realized by low achievers (1998b, p. 141). This was, and remains, powerful evidence for the value of formative assessment.

Based on their review, Black and Wiliam determined that effective formative assessment occurs

- when teachers make adjustments to teaching and learning in response to assessment information;

- when students receive feedback about their learning, with advice on what they can do to improve; and
- when students are involved in the process through peer and self-assessment.

Notice that Black and Wiliam refer to the "process" of formative assessment. Formative assessment is not a thing—it is not a single test given to students to see what they have learned for the purpose of grading, placement, or classification. That is the function of summative assessments like an end-of-unit classroom test, the quarterly benchmark test, or the annual state test. Instead, formative assessment is a process that occurs during teaching and learning and involves both teachers and students in gathering information so they can take steps to keep learning moving forward to meet the learning goals.

Lorrie Shepard, in her very influential 2000 presidential address to the American Educational Research Association, proposed a set of principles emerging from recent theories of learning as a framework to explain and integrate the findings from the diverse studies reviewed by Black and Wiliam. Among these were the following:

- Intellectual abilities are socially and culturally developed.
- Learners construct knowledge and understandings within a social context.
- Intelligent thought involves "metacognition" or self-monitoring of learning and thinking.
- New learning is shaped by prior knowledge and cultural perspectives.
- Deep learning is principled and supports transfer. (Shepard, 2000, p. 8)

She considered the kinds of assessment practices that are compatible with these principles, proposing fundamental changes in both the substance and purpose of assessments. In terms of substance, she argued that classroom assessments must be congruent with important learning goals, and they must directly connect to ongoing instruction. In terms of purpose, she called for fundamental changes in the perception of assessment functions. Assessments should be used to help students learn and to improve instruction, rather than functioning as "occasions for meting out rewards and punishment" (p. 10). Moreover, a reformed view of assessment should include not only clearly communicating expectations and intermediate steps to students, but also the requirement that students be actively involved in evaluating their own work (Shepard, 2000). Shepard's presidential address, with its recommendations for a revolution in attitudes toward assessment, placed a premium on the process of formative assessment for teaching and learning.

In this chapter, we will look at how the process of formative assessment works in the classroom, but first let's get into a little more detail about what formative assessment is. You can see several definitions of formative

What Experts Say About Formative Assessment

An assessment activity can help learning if it provides information to be used as feedback by teachers, and by their pupils in assessing themselves and each other, to modify the teaching and learning activities in which they are engaged. Such assessment becomes 'formative assessment' when the evidence is actually used to adapt teaching work to meet learning needs (Black, Harrison, Lee, Marshall, & Wiliam, 2003, p. 2).

The process used by teachers and students to recognize and respond to student learning in order to enhance that learning, during the learning (Bell & Cowie, 2001, p. 536).

Formative assessment is defined as assessment carried out during the instructional process for the purpose of improving teaching or learning (Shepard et al., 2005, p. 75).

Assessment for learning involves teachers in using a classroom assessment process to advance, not merely to check on learning (Stiggins, 2002, p. 5).

Formative assessment "takes place day by day and allows the teacher and the student to adapt their respective actions to the teaching/learning situation in question" (Allal & Lopez, 2005, p. 244).

Assessment for learning is the process of seeking and interpreting evidence for use by learners and their teachers to decide where the learners are in their learning, where they need to go and how best to get there (Assessment Reform Group, 2002, pp. 1–2).

Formative assessment is a planned process in which assessment-elicited evidence of students' status is used by teachers to adjust their ongoing instructional procedures or by students to adjust their current learning tactics (Popham, 2008, p. 6).

We see much more effective use of formative evaluation if it is separated from the grading process and used primarily as an aid to teaching (Bloom, 1969, p. 48).

assessment in the box above. Notice some of the key phrases these experts use in relation to formative assessment:

- *Information to be used as feedback by teachers and their pupils . . .*
- *Enhancing that learning during the learning . . .*
- *For the purpose of improving teaching and learning . . .*
- *Takes place day by day . . .*
- *Decide where pupils need to go and how to get there . . .*

- *Advance, not merely check on, student learning . . .*
- *By students to adjust their current learning tactics . . .*

The function of formative assessment as a means to improve learning during instruction clearly comes through, as does the idea that not only teachers but also students are active users of formative assessment. In sum, *formative assessment is a process that takes place continuously during the course of teaching and learning to provide teachers and students with feedback to close the gap between current learning and desired goals.*

THE PROCESS OF FORMATIVE ASSESSMENT

Now we are going to look closely at the process of formative assessment shown in Figure 2.1. Each element of the process is elaborated in subsequent chapters. What is important at this point is for you to gain an overview of the process and its components.

Note that the process is framed as a cycle, illustrating that formative assessment is *continuous* process, integrated into instruction. You'll also notice that the end point of the cycle is "close the gap." This is because formative assessment is intended to close the gap between where the learner currently is and where the learner and the teacher want to be at the end of a lesson. The idea of closing the "gap" comes from D. Royce Sadler (1989), who stressed feedback as the centerpiece of formative assessment. Following Ramaprasad (1983), he emphasized that information is only considered feedback when it is "used to alter the gap" (Sadler, 1989, p. 121). This means that the feedback generated from formative assessment must be used to make changes in the students' learning status and help them close the gap between their current status and the intended learning goal. When the gap is closed, another gap opens as student learning moves to the next stage, and formative assessment is used to close the gap once again.

DETERMINE LEARNING GOALS AND DEFINE CRITERIA FOR SUCCESS

The process of formative assessment begins (at the top left of Figure 2.1) with teachers identifying the learning goal(s) for a lesson or a sequence of lessons and determining the criteria for success. As Figure 2.1 suggests, the learning goal is derived from a learning progression (more on this in Chapter 4). The learning goal identifies what the students will learn during the course of the lesson or lessons. The success criteria identify what it

Figure 2.1 The Process of Formative Assessment

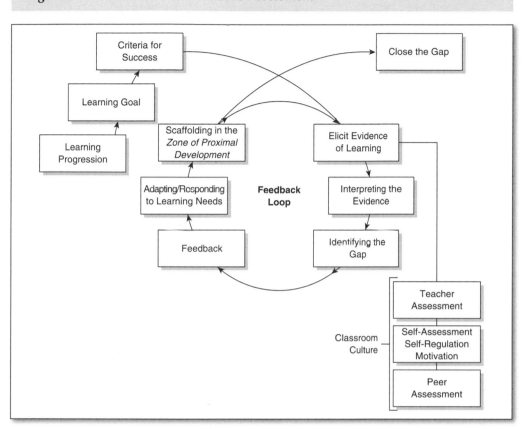

takes to meet the learning goal and are used as checks on learning. Before the lesson(s) begin, these goals and success criteria are shared with the students. Success criteria are the guide to learning *while* the student is engaged in the learning tasks.

ELICIT EVIDENCE OF LEARNING

While instruction is under way, teachers use a variety of strategies to elicit evidence of how student learning is evolving toward a goal. There is no single way to conduct formative assessment. Since 1969 when Bloom suggested the use of brief tests at the end of a phase of learning as an aid to teaching, the conception of formative assessment has enlarged. The enlarged perspective promotes the integration of formative assessment within each instructional activity, and therefore allows for more diversity in how learning is assessed. Diverse approaches can include, for example, planned questions, observation, instructional tasks (representations, explanation, performance, problem solving), exit cards, notes to the teacher, or curriculum-embedded assessments. The key point about the strategy employed is that it should enable teachers to access information about how learning is developing.

In general, strategies for eliciting evidence should be planned in advance of instruction, though sometimes they can arise spontaneously during the lesson. For example, when a teacher is planning a math lesson, she might decide on particular questions she will ask at specific points in the lesson to determine how well students understand the math concept, and adjust her instruction in light of the student response. However, in the same lesson spontaneous formative assessment can occur. This happens when the teacher gains an insight into student learning from something the students do or say during the instructional activity, sometimes referred to as a "teachable moment." In this case, too, the teacher will need to decide if any instructional adjustments are necessary. Chapter 5 will address in detail strategies to elicit evidence.

INTERPRETING THE EVIDENCE

Whether from planned or spontaneous formative assessment, teachers examine the evidence in relation to the success criteria to determine the status of student learning: what the students understand, what their misconceptions are, what knowledge they have or do not have, and what skills they are or are not acquiring. While interpreting evidence, the teacher may realize there is not enough evidence to make a determination about the students' current learning status, so eliciting further evidence will be necessary. The teacher might also find that they do not need to make any instructional adjustments because they have already met the success criteria.

While students are engaged in learning they use the success criteria to keep track of how well they are moving forward toward the goal, and to make adjustments to their learning when necessary. When students are involved in peer assessment, they also use the success criteria to interpret the evidence and provide each other with feedback about how learning can be improved. To do this, students must understand what the success criteria mean.

IDENTIFYING THE GAP

Recall that the purpose of formative assessment is to close the gap between students' current status and the intended learning goal. This is not the same as the "achievement gap" that describes the gap in achievement between some subgroups of students and others. Students who are learning something new *should* have a gap, otherwise learning is not advancing.

Interpreting the evidence from formative assessment is key to identifying the gap between students' current learning status and the goal of current instruction. Closing the gap is achieved by responding to the evidence through feedback, which results in adaptations to instruction and to learning.

FEEDBACK

To be effective in promoting learning, feedback needs to help students take steps to move forward in their learning. This does not mean telling the students if they are right or wrong. As Paul Black (2003) observes, this "is merely frequent summative assessment."

Instead, in formative assessment teachers provide descriptive feedback to the students about the status of their learning in relation to the success criteria and give cues to the students about what they can do to progress and close the gap. In a recent, extensive review of studies on feedback, Hattie and Timperley (2007) suggested that, whatever the source of the feedback, it must answer three major questions asked by a teacher and/or by a student:

- *Where am I going?* (What are the goals?)
- *How am I going?* (What progress is being made toward the goal?)
- *Where to next?* (What activities need to be undertaken to make better progress?) (p. 86)

Teachers are not the only ones to provide feedback. As noted earlier, peers can also provide feedback that helps their classmates improve learning. In addition to external feedback from teachers and peers, students get feedback about their own learning through self-assessment. This is important because when students are monitoring their learning they are engaged in metacognition (that is, thinking about thinking), which we know from cognitive research is important to effective thinking and competent performance (see, for example, National Research Council, 2000; National Research Council, 2001).

Sadler (1989) emphasized that to be able to self-monitor and engage in metacognitive activity, students must come to hold a conception of quality similar to the teacher's. He noted that to develop this concept of quality the student must:

- Possess a concept of the *standard* (or goal, or reference level) being aimed for,
- Compare the *actual* (or current) *level of performance* with the standard,
- Engage in appropriate *action* which leads to some closure of the gap. (Sadler, 1989, p. 121)

Later in the chapter, we will see what it means in practice to develop students' conceptions of quality so they can use feedback effectively to support their own learning.

The last thing to say about feedback here is that it must be *used* to improve learning. If feedback is not used it becomes in Sadler's terms "dangling data" and dangling data cannot close the gap, thus rendering the formative assessment process useless. Chapters 5 and 6 will focus on feedback.

ADAPTING AND RESPONDING TO LEARNING NEEDS

As a result of the feedback about learning teachers receive from formative assessment, they plan the action they will take so that their instruction is matched to the students' learning needs. In other words, teachers select learning experiences that will place appropriate demands on the students and lead to closing the gap between where the students currently are in learning and where they need to go.

By engaging in self-assessment, students also make adjustments to their own learning, selecting appropriate strategies from their repertoire so that they move forward. Chapter 6 deals with student self-assessment.

SCAFFOLDING NEW LEARNING

The term "scaffolding" characterizes the support that teachers (or peers) give to students to move them from what they already know to what they can do next and close the gap between their current learning status and the learning goal (Wood, Bruner, & Ross, 1976). The teacher provides the necessary instructional support so that learning is incrementally internalized, ultimately becoming part of the students' independent achievement, and thus closing the gap (Vygotsky, 1978). Students are responsive in the process of scaffolding, using feedback and their own learning strategies in collaboration with the teacher's instruction. Formative assessment takes place during scaffolding to identify the degree to which the learner is advancing and may result in further instructional/learning adaptations if the gap is not closing.

CLOSE THE GAP

The final step in the process of formative assessment is to close the gap between where learners are and where they need to be to achieve the learning goal. As one gap closes, the teacher selects new learning goals and another gap is created, renewing the formative assessment cycle.

CLASSROOM CULTURE

The whole process of formative assessment depends on a classroom culture where students feel safe to say they do not understand something and give and receive constructive feedback from peers. Teachers must establish a classroom culture characterized by a recognition and appreciation of individual differences. In a classroom where students listen respectfully to each other, respond positively and constructively, and appreciate the different skill levels among peers, all students will feel safe in the learning environment to learn with and from each other. We will discuss the classroom culture in greater detail in Chapter 7.

THEORY INTO PRACTICE

Now it's time to think about what the process of formative assessment looks like in practice. Consider this classroom scenario. In Mr. Gibson's tenth-grade English class, the students are working on developing a research paper. Mr. Gibson has told the students the learning goal they are currently focused on is the following:

> *To create a multi-genre paper informed by your research that presents one or more perspectives on a research question or thesis statement.*

Mr. Gibson has also provided the students with a set of criteria by which the quality of their paper will be judged:

1. The paper begins with a clear thesis statement.

2. The paper demonstrates a thorough knowledge of the topic.

3. Multiple genres are included.

4. Clear transitions are made between each genre.

5. The paper includes a series of claims and explanations.

To illustrate what the criteria look like before the students embark on their own paper, Mr. Gibson shares multi-genre papers written by his prior students. He asks students to work in pairs to discuss the papers and to think about where the papers meet the criteria, where they don't, and why. After the paired work, Mr. Gibson leads the students in a discussion of the criteria, asking pairs to share their thinking with the whole class. From this discussion, he is able to get a sense of how well the students understand the criteria and are able to clarify their thinking along the way.

During the time the students are creating their own paper, Mr. Gibson engages them in a range of activities, all consistent with the learning goal. First, the students write their individual thesis statement, and he provides written comments about its clarity as a beginning of the paper. In several cases, he makes suggestions for how the student might think about improving the statement. Next, the students develop an outline of the paper with a rationale for what information is important and why they have selected particular genres. The students share their outlines in groups of four, and peers provide comments on the outline and rationales for selection of information and genres. At this time, Mr. Gibson circulates around the classroom, listening to the discussion and intervening when he wants to clarify a point or probe the students' thinking.

Now, with a thesis statement and an outline of their paper, the students write a first draft. Mr. Gibson reminds them to constantly review their work in light of the criteria and exemplar papers he has provided, and to make adjustments when they think they are not successfully meeting any criterion. Once the first draft is completed, each student has a conference with a peer. The peers read each other's drafts against the criteria and provide comments about where they think the criteria have been met successfully, with suggestions for improvement. Then they go about revising their work to produce a second draft. At this point, they are ready for an individual conference with Mr. Gibson. To guide the conference, each student is required to submit their draft to him along with three specific questions. For example, one student has questions about the clarity of his thesis statement, about the degree to which his claims are backed by evidence, and the effectiveness of his use of transitions. To this student, Mr. Gibson provides the following feedback:

> *You have a clear thesis statement, and your paper provides a series of claims and examples. Your paper could be strengthened by improved use of transitions. I have marked places where you have used effective transitions with an X, and with a Z to indicate where transitions could be improved. Review the Xs to help you think about how to create better transitions in the Z sections, then we will discuss.*

After the students have received feedback from Mr. Gibson about their papers, they make revisions and resubmit them to him. Mr. Gibson reads and evaluates the final drafts and gives each paper a grade.

Let's think about this scenario in light of the research and theories presented earlier in the chapter. In Table 2.1, you can see the theory and how Mr. Gibson put it into practice.

Table 2.1 Theory Into Practice

Theory	*Practice*
Students developing the same conception of quality as the teacher (Black & Wiliam, 1998; Sadler, 1989). Students possess a concept of the *standard* (or goal, or reference level) being aimed for (Ramaprasad, 1983; Sadler, 1989). Learning expectations are visible to students (Shepard, 2000).	Mr. Gibson provides learning goal and criteria for meeting the goal. Teacher shares examples of prior students' work to illustrate criteria.
External feedback is provided (Black & Wiliam, 1998; Hattie & Timperley, 2007; Sadler, 1989). Feedback prompts an active response from students (Hattie & Timperley, 2007). Feedback is used to alter the gap between current status and reference level (Black & Wiliam, 1998; Bloom, 1969; Ramaprasad, 1983; Sadler, 1989).	Mr. Gibson writes comments on thesis statement, some students revise.
External feedback is provided (Hattie & Timperley, 2007; Ramaprasad, 1983; Sadler, 1989). Feedback prompts an active response from students (Black & Wiliam, 1998; Hattie & Timperley, 2007). Students are constructing knowledge within a social context (Shepard, 2000).	Students share outlines with peers who provide comments while Mr. Gibson observes.
Students are engaged in self-monitoring (Black & Wiliam, 1998; Sadler, 1989; Shepard, 2000).	Students write first draft monitoring their writing against the success criteria.
Feedback is used to alter the gap (Ramaprasad, 1983; Sadler, 1989).	Peers read first draft and provide comments against criteria. Revisions to paper.
Students are engaged in self-monitoring (Hattie & Timperley, 2007; Sadler, 1989; Shepard, 2000). Students use feedback to alter the gap between current status and reference level (Ramaprasad, 1983).	Mr.Gibson/student conference. Students bring up three questions about criteria to guide conference. Mr. Gibson provides comments.

In sum, Mr. Gibson presented the learning goals at the start of the instructional sequence and carried them through the sequence, making purposeful reference to them as appropriate. In addition, feedback was provided at multiple stages by both Mr. Gibson and peers. As the next section will illustrate, Mr. Gibson maintained a clear separation between formative and summative assessment functions.

FORMATIVE AND SUMMATIVE ASSESSMENT

What Experts Say About Summative and Formative Assessment

Formative assessment helps teachers adapt their instruction to meet students' needs and assists students to determine what learning adjustments they need to make. Summative assessment helps determine whether a student has reached a certain level of competency "after completing a particular phase of education, whether is be a classroom unit, or 12 years of schooling" (National Research Council, 2001, p. 38).

Summative assessments are used to measure what students have learned. Formative assessment refers to "frequent, interactive assessments of student progress and understanding to identify learning needs and adjust teaching appropriately" (Organisation for Economic Co-operation and Development, 2005, p. 21).

"Formative assessment is designed to extend and encourage learning; summative assessment is used to determine how much students have learned, with little or no emphasis on using results to improve learning." (McMillan, 2007, p. 7)

"Summative assessments are best thought of as retrospective. The vast majority of summative assessments in education are assessments of what the individual has learnt, know, understands and can do. In contrast, formative assessment can be thought of as being prospective." (Wiliam, 2000, p. 14)

In 1967, Michael Scriven used the terms "formative" and "summative" to describe the two distinct roles that evaluation of curriculum might play (Scriven, 1967, p. 43). He referred to the formative role of evaluation in relation to the "on-going improvement of the curriculum" (p. 41) and the summative role of evaluation serving to enable administrators to evaluate "the entire finished curriculum" (p. 42). In Scriven's view, formative evaluation would permit administrators to make ongoing improvements to the curriculum, and summative evaluation would occur at the point when administrators made a judgment about its quality. Since Scriven's original formulation, the terms summative and formative have been applied specifically to assessment. Summative assessment is concerned with summing up or summarizing the achievement status of a student. In contrast, formative assessment is concerned with how judgments about the quality of student responses (performances, pieces, or works) can be used to shape and improve student learning *during* the learning" (Bell & Cowie, 2001, p. 536; emphasis added).

As we saw earlier, Mr. Gibson provided a grade for the paper at the end of the process. His grade was a summative assessment of the final paper, his judgment about the level of performance the students had achieved. The grade did not provide feedback about how to improve, which as you recall is central to formative assessment.

When he was using formative assessment (the review of the thesis statement, the peer review of the outline, self-monitoring in relation to the success criteria and peer and teacher review of drafts), he received and provided feedback so he and his students could keep learning moving forward toward the ultimate goal.

In the next chapter, we will focus on where formative assessment fits in the big assessment picture and how both summative and formative can work together to contribute to effective teaching and learning.

SUMMING UP

- Formative assessment is used to make changes to alter the gap between current learning and desired goals.
- Formative assessment is a continuous process, integrated into instruction to collect evidence about *how* student learning is progressing toward learning goals.
- Formative assessment involves a variety of assessment methods and strategies—there is no one way to conduct formative assessment.
- Feedback that helps learners move forward is central to formative assessment.
- Formative assessment involves students in self-assessment about how their learning is progressing so that they can be active agents in learning, working with teachers to close the gap between current levels of understanding and desired learning goals.

REFLECTION QUESTIONS

1. How often do you use formative assessment in your classroom? How often do you use summative assessment?

2. For what purposes do you use summative and formative assessment? Are these purposes the same as the ones described in the chapter?

3. Which areas that you have read about in this chapter would you like to develop further in your work?

It All Depends on What the Data Tell You

"Cheshire . . . ," Alice began rather timidly, "would you tell me please, which way I ought to go from here?" "That all depends a good deal on where you want to get to," said the Cat.

—Lewis Carroll, *Alice's Adventures in Wonderland*

Perhaps the Cheshire Cat's answer to Alice's question should have been, "That all depends a good deal on what the data tell you." According to *Merriam-Webster's Eleventh Collegiate Dictionary* (2007), the word *data* is defined as "factual information (as measurement or statistics) used as a basis for reasoning, discussion or calculation" (p. 316). Teachers use different sources of assessment data to "reason" about student learning, to "discuss" what learning has been accomplished, and to "calculate" levels of achievement. In short, they use assessment data to draw inferences about learning to inform educational decisions.

Formative assessment functions as a component of a comprehensive assessment system. Formative assessment provides one source of data to inform educational decisions, specifically those decisions that guide instruction minute by minute, day by day (Leahy, Lyon, Thompson, & Wiliam, 2005). Other educational decisions are informed by different data sources, for example, data from the end-of-unit assessments or the end-of-year state tests. While all the remaining chapters focus exclusively on formative assessment, this chapter steps back to locate formative assessment in the larger assessment context.

We know from the field of educational measurement that "one assessment does not fit all" (National Research Council, 2001, p. 220). Different assessments have different purposes, and therefore they inform different decisions. In this chapter, we'll consider the various sources of assessment data available to teachers, what purposes they each serve, and how they inform a range of teacher decisions. When we are considering the array of available assessment data, we'll also be able to see where formative assessment fits into the big picture of assessment.

THE BIG ASSESSMENT PICTURE

In 2001, the authors of *Knowing What Students Know: The Science and Design of Educational Assessment* (*KWSK*) advanced a model for an assessment system to serve multiple, decision-making purposes (National Research Council, 2001). The authors proposed that such systems should be *coherent, comprehensive,* and *continuous (3Cs).*

- A *coherent* assessment system is built on a well-structured conceptual base—an expected learning progression, which serves as the foundation of all assessments.
- A *comprehensive* assessment system "provides a variety of evidence to support educational decision making." (p. 259)
- A *continuous* assessment system provides "indications of student growth over time." (p. 259)

In Figure 3.1, we can see what a system characterized by the 3Cs might look like: a range of assessments, from minute by minute to the annual state assessments, providing different levels of detail about student learning over time to be used for various decision-making purposes.

Figure 3.1 Sources of Assessment Data

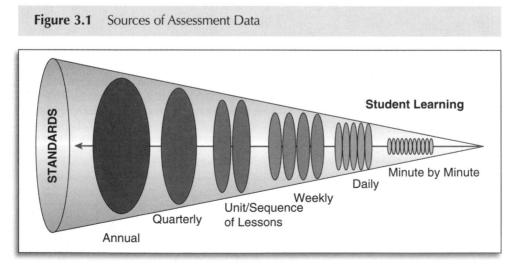

SOURCE: Adapted from Herman & Heritage, 2007.

While we remain at some distance from a comprehensive system built on the same underlying model of learning advocated by *KWSK,* nonetheless the framework set forth there helps us think about the different purposes assessments can serve. Taken together, all assessments in the system should provide a continuous picture of student learning, yielding data about the extent to which students have met or are on the way to meeting learning goals. Later in the chapter, we will look at the different assessments shown in Figure 3.1, but first, we need to consider the all-important issue in educational assessment: appropriateness for purpose. Or put another way, which assessments in the system are appropriate for each of the decisions teachers need to make?

APPROPRIATENESS FOR PURPOSE

The most important question teachers need to answer when they are using assessment data is "Do these data come from assessments that are appropriate to purpose?" Teachers need to know that the inferences they draw from the data are valid, and inferences will not be valid if the assessments are not appropriate to purpose.

Validity is the key issue in educational measurement. Validity refers to whether an assessment is measuring what it is intended to measure and can well serve the intended purpose. Validity is always related to a specific use of the assessment or the interpretation of the data yielded by the assessment (American Educational Research Association, American Psychological Association, & National Council on Measurement in Education, 1999).

What an assessment measures is termed a *construct.* A construct is the specific characteristic—for instance, the ability, skill, understanding, psychological trait, or personal quality—that the test is intended to measure. For example, reading comprehension, number sense, and scientific inquiry are all constructs. When teachers are using assessment results, they need to be sure that the assessment is measuring the construct they think it is measuring. Otherwise, the inferences they draw from the data may be inaccurate and lead to inappropriate decisions. For example, if the assessment is intended to measure students' reading comprehension, then it must measure the range of abilities, skills, and understandings comprising the construct of reading comprehension. If it only measures decoding skills or vocabulary, then teachers may draw inferences about students' decoding skills or vocabulary knowledge. However, they will not be able to draw inferences about students' reading comprehension because the decoding and vocabulary constructs do not comprise the full range of abilities, skills, and understanding comprising the reading comprehension construct.

Assessment reliability is another important issue in educational measurement. Reliability refers to how consistently an assessment measures what it is intended to measure (American Educational Research Association, American Psychological Association, & National Council on Measurement in Education, 1999). If a test is reliable, the results should be repeatable. For instance, changes in the time of administration, day and time of scoring, who scores the assessment, and changes in the sample of assessment items should not create inconsistencies in results. Reliability is important because it is necessary for assessment validity. If assessment results are not consistent, then we can conclude that the results are not accurate measurements of what the assessment is intended to measure.

Validity and reliability are important issues for *all* assessments, but particularly for those assessments where the consequences of student performance are very high—for example, the annual state tests that can have significant consequences such as student retention. These kinds of high-stakes tests will have (or should have) undergone a rigorous process to establish their technical quality. Establishing technical quality involves accumulating validity and reliability evidence to support the use of the assessment for the intended purpose. All the assessments shown in Figure 3.1 should be valid and reliable. In Chapter 5, we will discuss the issues of validity and reliability as they apply to formative assessment that is integrated into instruction—in particular for those assessments that occur minute by minute or daily—where the consequences for an inaccurate inference are not very great. If teachers make a mistake one day, there is a good chance this can be rectified by the inference they draw the next.

However, at the very minimum, all assessments, formative, benchmark, progress monitoring, or accountability, should be aligned to learning goals, be they long term or short term. Within this array, the purpose of formative assessment is to promote further learning. In this vein, Stobart (2006) has argued that overriding concern in the validity of formative assessment is consequential validity; in other words, does the use of the assessment result in effective learning in subsequent instruction? According to Stobart, absent consequential validity, formative assessment does not and cannot meet validity standards.

Now that we have established the importance of the ideas of validity and reliability in assessment, let's take a look at processes teachers can use to make sense of the data to make them usable in the classroom.

MAKING SENSE OF THE DATA

Teachers have to make sense of the data to render them usable in the classroom. Figure 3.2 shows four steps teachers can follow to make sense of the data.

Figure 3.2   Steps to Make Sense of Data

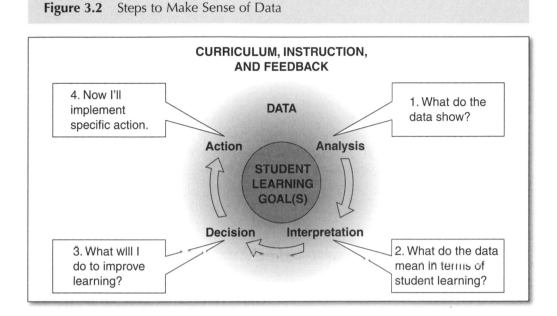

Curriculum, instruction, and feedback are the means teachers use to assist students to reach learning goals. Either during the course of learning or after a period of learning, assessment data are gathered to evaluate the learning that is either developing or has been achieved. Teachers then analyze what the data show and interpret what they mean in terms of student learning. For example, from annual state assessments teachers might see that a large number of students have scored below basic in a strand of mathematics and might infer that they have a weakness in this particular area. However, we should inject a word of caution here about drawing inferences concerning either strengths or weaknesses from one assessment, especially if there are only a few items to measure the construct. Before jumping to any conclusions, teachers must look for corroborating evidence, for example, from other assessments or analysis of student work. With enough corroborating evidence in hand to support their inferences, teachers then come to a conclusion about what kind of decisions they will make to further learning based on their interpretation. Finally, they have to implement their decision and take action.

Of course the time frame for analyzing and interpreting the data, making decisions, and taking action will vary according to the purpose of the assessment. For example, decisions about program or curricular changes might occur from the analysis and interpretation of annual state tests and other kinds of benchmark tests, while decisions about what to do in the next lesson could result from the minute-by-minute or daily assessment of learning.

DIFFERENT ASSESSMENTS FOR DIFFERENT PURPOSES

As we have already discussed, assessments shown in Figure 3.1 serve different purposes. Each one covers different-sized chunks of learning, ranging from learning occurring on a minute-by-minute basis, to the cumulative learning that has taken place over the course of a year, which is sampled by the annual state assessments.

To provide a coherent picture of learning, all the chunks, regardless of size, should be connected together in a clear progression of learning. Essentially, each learning chunk is made up of the subgoals of the next, larger chunk. Subgoals are the building blocks that enable students to meet longer-term goals. For example, small chunks of learning occurring over a lesson or several lessons should be connected to the larger chunk of a unit, the larger chunk of a unit connected to the chunk of learning that takes place over a quarter, and the even larger chunks of quarterly learning need to connect to the ultimate goals, the state standards. Ideally, the standards themselves should be connected so they provide a clear and coherent picture of the knowledge, concepts and skills students need to acquire over the course of their schooling.

As we stated earlier, the assessments in the system need to align to the learning goals of the different learning chunks to provide teachers with the range of information they need. Because they are aligned to different-sized chunks of learning, they provide different levels of detail. For example, by their very nature annual state tests can only provide a gross measure of learning. In contrast, minute-by-minute or daily assessments provide a much greater level of detail. So how do the differences in the grain size of these different levels of information contribute to differences in the use teachers can make of the various assessments? In the next section, we'll answer that question.

DIFFERENT GRAIN SIZES

In Figure 3.3, we can see a representation of assessments of different levels of granularity and the kinds of questions that teachers can ask of the each data source to get information about student learning.

The questions guide teachers' process of "reasoning, discussion, and calculation." Once teachers have concluded this process—in other words, once they have drawn inferences from the results —they need to decide on and then take various courses of action. Without action, the data serve no purpose, and merely become, in Sadler's (1989) term, "dangling data" (p. 121)—knowledge

Figure 3.3 Assessments of Different Grain Sizes for Different Purposes

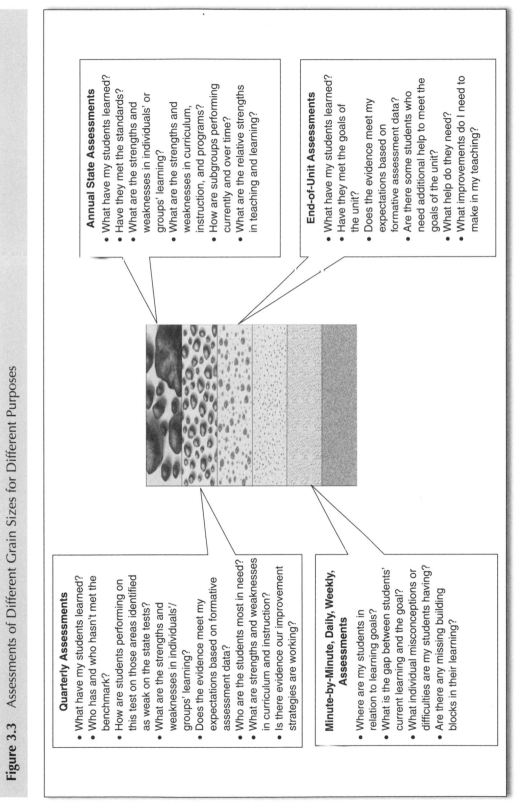

Annual State Assessments
- What have my students learned?
- Have they met the standards?
- What are the strengths and weaknesses in individuals' or groups' learning?
- What are the strengths and weaknesses in curriculum, instruction, and programs?
- How are subgroups performing currently and over time?
- What are the relative strengths in teaching and learning?

End-of-Unit Assessments
- What have my students learned?
- Have they met the goals of the unit?
- Does the evidence meet my expectations based on formative assessment data?
- Are there some students who need additional help to meet the goals of the unit?
- What help do they need?
- What improvements do I need to make in my teaching?

Quarterly Assessments
- What have my students learned?
- Who has and who hasn't met the benchmark?
- How are students performing on this test on those areas identified as weak on the state tests?
- What are the strengths and weaknesses in individuals'/ groups' learning?
- Does the evidence meet my expectations based on formative assessment data?
- Who are the students most in need?
- What are strengths and weaknesses in curriculum and instruction?
- Is there evidence our improvement strategies are working?

Minute-by-Minute, Daily, Weekly, Assessments
- Where are my students in relation to learning goals?
- What is the gap between students' current learning and the goal?
- What individual misconceptions or difficulties are my students having?
- Are there any missing building blocks in their learning?

of students recorded somewhere in some system, not knowledge that teachers and students can use to inform next steps in learning.

Let's now look at the actions teachers might take from each source of data.

TAKING ACTION

Figure 3.4 shows the action that can result from analyzing and interpreting the data from each type of assessment.

WHERE DOES FORMATIVE ASSESSMENT FIT IN?

So far, we have learned about different assessments for different purposes and the decisions about learning each assessment can inform. Now we are going to look specifically at where formative assessment fits in. Recall the definition of formative assessment presented in Chapter 2:

> *Formative assessment is a process that takes place continuously during the course of teaching and learning to provide teachers and students with feedback to close the gap between current learning and desired goals.*

In formative assessment, teachers collect data while learning is taking place. Formative assessment strategies are aligned to the short-term subgoals, which are the focus of the lesson, and data from them provide teachers with a steady stream of information to keep learning moving forward. While teachers get fine-grained information from formative assessment to guide teaching and learning day by day, other assessments linked to longer-term goals provide snapshots of progress on the way to meeting standards. The important point here is that the short-term goals should be subgoals of the longer-term goals so that all the assessments in the system are providing a coherent picture of learning.

The effective use of formative assessment depends on the judgments teachers make about the data and the action they take based on those judgments. If the learning goals of each lesson are subgoals of the teacher's longer-term learning goals, the formative assessment strategies are aligned with the subgoals, and the teacher judgments are accurate, there really should be no surprises in the data from the assessments that provide snapshots of progress toward the larger goals. Either way, in addition to using other assessments to check on progress, teachers can also use them to check on their own judgments in formative assessment, assuming that the calibrating assessments are of high enough technical quality.

Figure 3.4   Action From Assessments of Different Grain Sizes

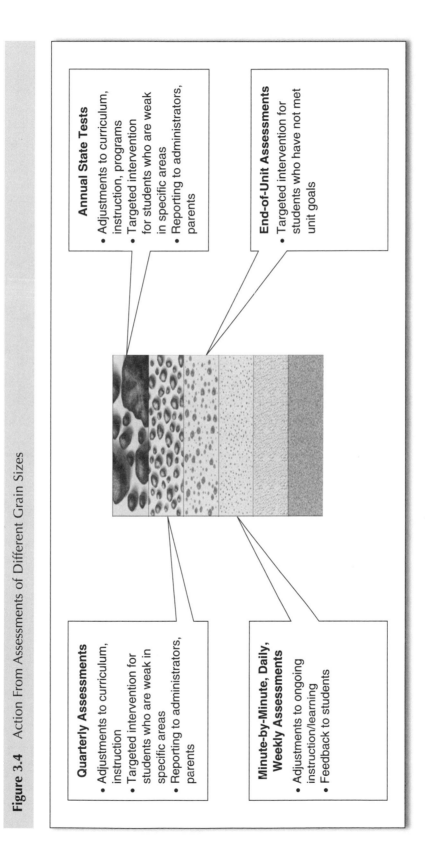

Annual State Tests
- Adjustments to curriculum, instruction, programs
- Targeted intervention for students who are weak in specific areas
- Reporting to administrators, parents

End-of-Unit Assessments
- Targeted intervention for students who have not met unit goals

Quarterly Assessments
- Adjustments to curriculum, instruction
- Targeted intervention for students who are weak in specific areas
- Reporting to administrators, parents

Minute-by-Minute, Daily, Weekly Assessments
- Adjustments to ongoing instruction/learning
- Feedback to students

PUTTING IT ALL TOGETHER

To help illustrate how teachers can use the different assessments available to them, we turn to the fourth-grade teachers at Harrison Elementary School. What is important to note from the outset is that although this scenario is from an elementary school, it is equally applicable to middle and high schools. Grade-level groups or even whole departments could come together and engage in the same practices we will see at Harrison Elementary.

These teachers are using the results of statewide tests, summative data, to begin to answer the questions: "What have my students already learned?" and "Have they met the standards?"

It is the middle of June and the fourth-grade teachers are meeting to prepare for the upcoming school year. The teachers, who are gathered around a table in the teachers' lounge, are examining a report they generated from their districtwide database. They want the answer to the question: "How well did this year's third-grade students perform on the statewide reading assessment?" As they review the report, the teachers notice that about half of their incoming fourth-grade students score in the advanced and proficient categories for reading, and half score in the basic and below basic categories. Already, the teachers have a sense of the work cut out for them in the coming school year, and they are anxious to get more detailed information to help them understand student needs more fully.

The teachers get more information from statewide tests in answer to their question "What have my students already learned?"

The teacher leading the meeting, Ms. Watson, then proposes they look at the student performance by the subscales of the test. The others agree, and she quickly queries the database and generates another report. The teachers examine the report and see that students who scored at the "basic" and "below basic" levels performed well in word analysis but were weaker in vocabulary and reading comprehension.

So far the teachers have used data from the annual state tests, which are summative assessments. These assessments will have undergone a rigorous process to establish their validity and reliability—two central aspects of their technical quality. They examined aggregated data, which is when student data is combined so that individual performance or performance of particular groups cannot be identified. The aggregated data they reviewed showed a summary of the performance of *all* the incoming fourth-grade students on the statewide assessment. From this aggregated, summative data, the teachers were able to get an idea of the overall levels of achievement in reading of their incoming students, as measured by the assessment. As well as the aggregated achievement levels, they were also able to look at the subscales of the test, results of the items that test specific areas—in this case, the items testing vocabulary, word analysis, and reading comprehension—to find more information about strengths and weaknesses.

It is worth noting that when the third-grade teachers look back at the results of this test to answer the questions "What are the strengths and weaknesses in curriculum and instruction?" and "How can I improve my teaching?," they will have the same information about their own students' performance to give some guidance about improvements they could make to curriculum and instruction for the next year's third-grade students. Now let's return to the fourth-grade teacher meeting.

Once the teachers have reviewed the subscales, Ms. Watson says, "I suggest we look at the student scores on the school's quarterly district reading inventory to see how much progress these students made over the year,

> The teachers are using more than one measure to check for corroborating evidence of achievement.

and to see if the same patterns show up as we see on the state test subscales." Reviewing the line graph, showing the four data points, the teachers notice that while student vocabulary and comprehension skills improved over the previous school year, the growth of these skills was still slower than growth in word analysis skills. "So we are seeing the same pattern in these results as we did in the state test results," says Ms. Chapman. Ms. Watson agrees that they are seeing the same results and adds that they are making a good start on getting a handle on where are students are in reading and deciding the focus for their planning to begin the year.

At the end of their meeting, the teachers decide to repeat the same process to examine the assessment results of the specific students who will be in their classes the next school year. Individually, they examine aggregated class performance on the state test, then performance by subscales, and finally, they look at student performance on the quarterly district assessments. The teachers share their findings at the following grade-level meeting a week later. Toward the end of the meeting Ms. Watson sums up: "It seems that in general the individual class findings reflect those of the grade level. But there are some definite differences among our classes." Ms. Hamley notes it was really clear from the reading inventory data that some of the individual students in each class have specific needs, particularly in her class and Ms. Chapman's class with predicting and summarizing and that they are going to need a lot of help.

What have the teachers done so far in their meetings? They have used two sources of summative assessment data: one source to give them information about levels of performance students had reached in reading at the end of the school year; the other source to show achievement at four points throughout the year, and from which they could see students' growth trajectory in reading. From these data, the teachers were able to answer the questions:

- What have my students learned?
- What are the strengths and weaknesses in individual's and groups' learning?
- What are the differences among groups?

At this point, the teachers have a sense of the strengths and weaknesses of their incoming students and are able to begin some program planning for the start of the next school year. However, once the students begin school, they plan to use additional fine-grained assessment to have more detailed information about individual student's needs.

We know from cognitive research the importance of prior knowledge to learning. Effective teachers identify student prior knowledge and build on it to make connections to new learning (National Research Council, 2000). At the start of the school year, the teachers continue their investigation about student prior knowledge and are still focused on the question, "What have my students learned?" The answers will provide the basis for understanding the needs of individuals and groups more fully, and enable teachers to plan instruction accordingly. Let's return to the teachers and see what they do to gather more information.

Each of the fourth-grade teachers has a plan for how they are going to get more fine-grained information about their students' knowledge and skills in reading so they can match their instruction to the learning needs. Among the strategies they use to elicit the information are:

- Visualization—drawing pictures and diagrams of their understanding of their ideas in text with explanations
- Write questions that will test their understanding of a passage
- Explain and show how to clarify meaning, for example, using commas or conjunctions as guides to where the author provides definitions of words that may be unfamiliar to the reader
- Summarize—telling the most important ideas in two or three sentences

- Write or tell what they already know from the text and writing or telling some questions that still need to be answered in the subsequent text
- Make predictions in response to questions based on the questions
- Read a passage and infer two things that were not explicitly stated in the text: Explain the reasons for their inferences

The teachers use the data from these strategies to corroborate the information about the students' skills they received from their analysis of assessment data. They do this because they know the value of data from multiple measures for decision making. Multiple measures increase the validity and reliability of the teachers' interpretations. The teachers are also aware that the students' reading status may have changed somewhat over the summer—students may have increased their skills through practicing reading or other interventions, but they may have also lost some of their skills. Either way, to ensure valid and reliable inferences of students' current reading levels, it is important to check exactly where the students are.

> The teachers are collecting information to answer the questions: "Where are my students in relation to learning goals?," "What is the gap between students' current learning and the goal?," and "How do I keep learning moving forward?"

Not only do the teachers use these strategies to elicit detailed prior knowledge, but they continue to use the same strategies to give them fine-grained data to guide ongoing teaching and learning.

At their grade-level meetings they share strategies to elicit ongoing evidence. Ms. Hamley tells the group that today she tried something she hadn't done before which gave her valuable information. She asked a group of students to tell her what they already knew from part of a chapter they had read and then to write some questions that still needed to be answered. She reported that she could really see Ryan's problem with prediction because he wasn't able to clearly state what was already known and relate it to what he still needed to know. Ms. Ross wondered if Hailey had the same problem and told the group that she would try the same strategy with her.

Throughout the first quarter, the teachers use ongoing, frequent formative assessment. With this evidence, they are able to determine what the next steps in learning should be, anticipating that adjustments to teaching and learning made on the basis of the evidence should result in improved learning. And, of course, if it does not, they will use other formative assessment strategies to figure out why no improvement has occurred and what alternative action can be taken. In their classrooms, the process of using formative assessment is continuous: assess, make adjustments, assess again, make adjustments, and so on.

Toward the end of the quarter, the teachers administer the schoolwide reading inventory. The results from this assessment provide answers to these questions:

- What have my students learned?
- Who has and who hasn't met the benchmark?
- How are students performing on those areas identified as weak on the state tests?
- What are the strengths and weaknesses in individual's/groups' learning?
- Does the evidence meet my expectations based on formative assessment data?
- Who are the students most in need?
- What are strengths and weaknesses in curriculum and instruction?
- Is there evidence our teaching strategies are working?

Returning to the teachers we'll see how they use this information at their grade-level meeting to review the results from the assessment.

Ms. Watson begins, "You know, we always look at the results, but really because we continuously assess our students, we are usually not surprised by the results. We already have a good idea of where are students are." "That's right," responds Ms. Chapman. "But I always feel like it is a good check. I see it as another source of evidence that is useful—it gives me a sense of whether my instruction is on the right track." First, the teachers review the overall grade-level results, and they are pleased to see that there has been improvement in areas that showed up as weak when they analyzed the state assessment data before the start of the school year. Then together they review the results from each class. They notice that Ms. Hamley's students have made considerable improvement in summarizing and predicting. All the teachers are impressed by the improvement, and a discussion ensues where Ms. Hamley shares some of the assessment and instructional strategies she has used.

The teachers' use of frequent, fine-grained information from formative assessment goes on throughout the next quarter. At the end of the quarter, teachers examine the schoolwide reading assessment again. They continue the same process until the end of year. By the time they have the results of the last quarter's reading assessment, they feel confident about the progress the students have made. Indeed, when they examine the results they are very pleased with the outcome. "I feel really good about what we have accomplished this year with these students. Across the board, they have made progress," comments Ms. Ross. "Yes, I think that's true," says Ms. Chapman. "The program planning we did at the start of the year has paid off."

"It's not just that, though," adds Ms. Hamley. "We've really done a good job of keeping track of our students throughout the quarter—that's also made a big contribution." The teachers note the gains that have been made and also discuss the rate of progress. This leads to a discussion about the program and whether certain elements should have been emphasized more. Ms. Watson makes a suggestion: "Before we go much further in thinking about the year and the program, I'd like to wait until we get the state test results. I want to find out if we are seeing the same things in the state test results as we are here—we'll have more to go on." There is general agreement about Ms. Watson's idea. When the teachers get the results of the state tests they engage in a review of their own program and instruction—what worked, what didn't, and what they could do to improve?

The teachers have now come full circle. Not only do they use the fourth-grade assessment results to evaluate their instruction, but they also use the third-grade results to engage in planning for the next year, just as they did the previous year.

What have we learned from these fourth-grade teachers' use of data?

✓ **Data use matters:**

The teachers worked together, analyzing data with the goal of taking action to improve student learning. They collaborated to plan the curriculum and instructional practices, and they learned from each other about what works.

✓ **One size does not fit all:**

The fourth-grade teachers used a variety of assessments to gauge student learning. Each of the assessments had a different purpose, ranging from assessments to determine proficiency levels (have my students met the standards?), to indicate progress (are my students making progress?), and to guide day-to-day instruction (how do I keep learning moving forward?)

✓ **Data use is ongoing:**

For these teachers, data use is not a single event. Rather, it is a coordinated and systematic approach for analyzing different sources of data to improve learning. Particularly important is the use of fine-grained formative data to guide ongoing teaching and learning.

Formative assessment should be part of a coordinated system of assessment that provides teachers with data to inform the different decisions they need to make to support learning. As we saw at Harrison Elementary, the teachers used all the assessments in the system and moved back and forth from the large grain size—what achievement for students looked like over time (e.g., quarterly and annual assessments)—to the finer grain size— what achievement needed to look like for the students the very next minute or next day.

In the next chapter, we are going to look closely at how teachers determine the small chunks of learning that they assess through the process of formative assessment.

SUMMING UP

- Different assessments have different purposes, and they inform different educational decisions.
- Validity is the key issue in educational measurement.
- Reliability is a necessary but insufficient condition for validity.
- When teachers are making decisions based on assessment results, they need to be sure that the assessment is measuring the construct they think it is measuring.
- Teachers should not jump to conclusions about student learning based on the results of one assessment. Multiple measures are needed.
- To provide a coherent picture of learning, all the subgoals or chunks of learning, regardless of size, should be connected together in a clear progression of learning.
- Assessments must be aligned with learning goals.

REFLECTION QUESTIONS

1. How does what you now do in your classroom to assess student learning compare with what has been presented in the chapter?

2. How do you know that the assessments you use are valid and reliable?

3. What are your strengths in assessing student learning, and which areas that you have read about in this chapter would you like to develop further?

4

The Drivers of Formative Assessment

Learning Goals and Success Criteria

In Chapter 2, we learned that D. Royce Sadler specified three interrelated conditions for formative assessment. These were that teachers and students must

- possess a concept of the *standard* (or goal, or reference level) being aimed for;
- compare the *actual* (or current) *level of performance* with the standard; and
- engage in appropriate *action* which leads to some closure of the gap (Sadler, 1989, p. 121).

To meet these conditions, teachers and students need to be clear about the learning goal—what is to be learned—and also to have a clear conception of what it means to meet the learning goal—the criteria for success. Essentially, the learning goals and success criteria drive the whole process of formative assessment. They establish what learning is being aimed for, they enable teachers and students to compare actual levels of learning with the goal, and in so doing generate feedback to move toward meeting the goal.

In this chapter, we will explore how learning goals and success criteria drive the process of formative assessment, how they are derived, and how they are used as the interpretive framework for the evidence elicited from formative assessment. We begin with the important concept of learning progressions as a means to clarify goals.

First, what are learning progressions, how do they support developing learning goals and the process of formative assessment, and how are they created?

What Experts Say About Learning Goals

Goals help people focus on the task, select and apply appropriate strategies, and monitor goal progress (Schunk, 1995).

Goals that incorporate specific performance standards are more likely to enhance self-regulation and activate self-evaluations than are such general goals as "do my best" or "try hard" (Locke & Latham, 1990).

Proximal, short-term goals result in higher motivation and better self-regulation than more distant, long-term goals (Bandura, 1997; Boekaerts, Pintrich, & Zeidner, 2000; Locke & Latham, 1990).

Specific learning goals focus students' attention, and feedback can be directed to them. The goals and associated feedback include information about the criteria for success in attaining them (Hattie & Timperley, 2007).

"Those motivated by goals identified in terms of learning apply effort in acquiring new skills, seek to understand what is involved rather than just committing information to memory, persist in the face of difficulties, and generally try to increase their competence." (Harlen, 2006, p. 65)

LEARNING PROGRESSIONS

By its very nature, learning involves progression. To assist in its emergence, teachers need to understand the pathways along which students are expected to progress. These pathways or progressions ground both instruction and formative assessment. As Black and Wiliam (1998a) noted, teachers need

> to develop methods to interpret and respond to the results in a formative way. One requirement for such an approach is a sound model

of students' progression in the learning of the subject matter, so that the criteria that guide the formative strategy can be matched to students' trajectories of learning. (p. 37)

However, despite a plethora of standards and curricula, we lack good road maps that describe the trajectories of learning in specific domains. Why is this the case?

The Committee on Science Learning K–8 (National Research Council, 2007) offered a telling diagnosis:

Many standards and curricula contain too many disconnected topics that are given equal priority. The way many standards and curricula are conceived limits their utility for planning instruction and assessing learning. Too little attention is given to how students' understanding of a topic can be supported from grade to grade. (p. 231)

Although the authors are referring specifically to science, this charge can be leveled equally at other domains.

Even though meeting standards is the ultimate goal of instruction, most state standards do not provide clear progressions that allow teachers and students to locate where students are on the pathway to desired learning goals. In fact, many state standards lack the clarity to provide a definite picture of what learning is expected. In the main, they consist of propositional knowledge for different ages, without providing operational definitions of understanding (Smith, Wiser, Anderson, & Krajcik, 2006). While most existing standards describe what students should learn, by a certain grade level "they do not describe how students learn in ways that are maximally useful for curriculum and instruction" (National Research Council, 2001, p. 256). It is fair to say that if the standards do not present clear descriptions of how student learning progresses in a domain, then they are unlikely to be useful for formative assessment.

Standards are insufficiently clear about how learning develops for teachers to be able to map formative assessment opportunities to them. This means that teachers are not able to determine where student learning lies on a continuum and to know what to do to plan next steps to keep learning moving forward. Explicit learning progressions can provide the clarity that teachers need. By describing a pathway of learning, they can assist teachers to plan instruction. Formative assessment can be tied to learning goals, and the evidence elicited can be used to determine students' understanding and skill at a given point. When teachers understand the continuum of learning in a domain and have information about current status relative to learning goals, they are better able to make decisions about what the next steps in learning should be.

There are a number of reasons why many curricula are also problematic for planning learning and formative assessment. Curricula are often organized around scope and sequence charts that specify procedural objectives to be mastered at each grade. Usually, these are discrete objectives and not connected to each other in a larger network of organizing concepts (National Research Council, 2000). In this context, rather than providing details about the status of the student's learning relative to the desired learning goal (the hallmark of formative assessment) so that pedagogical decisions can be made, assessment will be summative and related to how well the student completed the task. Textbooks too can suffer from the same problems.

Ideally, learning progressions should be developed from a strong research base about the structure of knowledge in a discipline and about how learning occurs. Yet, the research base in many areas is not as robust as it might be. Current research only defines how a limited number of areas can be divided into learning progressions (Herman, 2006). Teachers cannot wait for the research community to catch up. They need better examples of how learning develops than those currently available. So how can teachers construct learning progressions to help them plan instruction and formative assessment?

In the next sections, we will look at how teachers developed a learning progression for an area of reading and for a strand of mathematics to assist them with instructional planning and formative assessment.

DEVELOPING A LEARNING PROGRESSION FOR READING

The first example of developing a learning progression comes from a group of teachers from Wisconsin. They began from the state standard for reading:

- Use effective reading strategies to achieve their purposes in reading

And the standard's subcomponent:

- Use a variety of strategies and word recognition skills, including rereading, finding context clues, applying knowledge of letter-sound relationships, and analyzing word structures

Working collaboratively, they identified the subconcepts and subskills that would lead to understanding of the concepts or acquisition of the skills represented in the subcomponent of the standard. To identify these subskills, the group drew from their combined expertise of working with students, and from their knowledge of the substantial body of literature on reading development. In the case of *analyzing word structure,* for instance, the subskills identified were use of knowledge of regular letter/sound correspondences to analyze words; use of knowledge of irregular spelling patterns, diphthongs, and digraphs; and use of knowledge of prefixes, affixes, suffixes, and inflections to read words.

Once the teams had decided on the key subconcepts or subskills, they laid them out in a progression that made sense in terms of what they knew about learning and instruction. For this process, they used sticky notes so that they could move around the sequence as ideas were discussed in the group. They spent time discussing the appropriate level of detail for the subconcepts and subskills in the progression. Teams decided that the issue of the necessary level of detail could not be resolved at this stage in development, and the progression would be adjusted when experience with it showed what subconcepts and skills were providing too little or too much information to be helpful for instruction and formative assessment. Once the initial progression was completed, the following questions prompted further discussion and planning:

- Are the major building blocks (i.e., critical concepts/skills) in the learning progression addressed?
- Are they linked in way that helps build understanding and skills?
- Do other teachers agree with this description of the progression?
- What is the research evidence for this progression of learning?

The teachers also intended to use these questions to review the progression at regular intervals when they had the benefit of implementation experience.

Although the process started with individual grade-level standards, eventually the teachers developed a K–12 progression with the standards functioning as the "benchmarks" along the way. In this way, rather than simply identifying chunks of a progression for each standard, teachers ended up with a multiyear trajectory of learning that permitted integration across year groups, and which they could use for planning instruction and formative assessment. As the leader of one of the teams commented:

We have done backward design planning in our district for many years, but this process gave us the missing piece. Focusing on the important building blocks is what we needed. We can see what we need to teach and to assess.

DEVELOPING A LEARNING PROGRESSION FOR MATHEMATICS

A group of teachers in New York State followed the same process as teachers in Wisconsin, but this time for an area of mathematics. They started with a focus on the state standards for measurement:

- Select tools and units (customary and metric) appropriate for the length measured;
- Use a ruler to measure to the nearest standard unit (whole, ½ and ¼ inches, whole feet, whole yards, whole centimeters, and whole meters); and
- Know and understand equivalent standard units of length: 12 inches = 1 foot, 3 feet = 1 yard.

Working in teams, they defined a progression for measurement. They divided their progression into three complementary and overlapping strands: vocabulary, concepts, and skills. For example, comparative language such as long, longer, longest, concepts such as a unit as the basis of the measurement system, and skills like measuring with accuracy. They thought about the antecedent understanding and skills students would need before they could meet these standards and also went much further in the progression than the level of competence represented in the standard.

Almost immediately, the teachers realized they could not teach measurement in isolation. In particular, measurement concepts needed to be developed hand in hand with number concepts. So they created an underlying number strand. In Figure 4.1, to the right you can see the measurement progression they developed. Underneath the strip labeled "Measurement Concepts," the teachers placed sticky notes to show a complementary strand for number. For example, one of the measurement concepts the teachers wanted students to understand was units can have fractional relationships. So they decided they would use measurement to teach fraction concepts.

We can learn from the New York teachers' experience that even though we might want to consider a learning progression for a strand in isolation, in fact, progressions will most likely overlap or intertwine with other strands in the domain. In relation to science, for example, Stevens, Shin, Delgado, Krajcik, and Pellegrino (2007) defined learning progressions, as "strategic sequencing that promotes both branching out and forming connections between ideas related to a core scientific concept or big idea" (p. 4). In reading, the strands of phonological awareness, decoding skills, sight

Figure 4.1   Measurement Progression

recognition of familiar words, background knowledge of the subject of the text, receptive and expressive vocabulary, knowledge of grammatical structures, inferential skills, and knowledge of different styles of discourse, including different genres (e.g., narrative, expository) are interrelated (Scarborough, 2001). So when teachers are constructing learning progressions, it will be important for them to decide what is the pathway for the strand along which students are expected to progress, as well as other complementary strands that may need to be addressed as students make progress in the domain.

At the time of writing, Common Core Standards are under development. These are essential standards that describe the most important knowledge, concepts, and skills students need to acquire to be successful in the global economy and as citizens of the United States of America. Let us hope these standards more clearly define pathways of learning than current standards so that teachers have what they need to plan instruction and formative assessment to keep learning moving forward.

LEARNING GOALS AND SUCCESS CRITERIA

Once teachers have a clear conception of the expected progression of learning, they can identify learning goals from the progression. Learning goals specify the learning that is intended (and are sometimes referred to as learning intentions) for a lesson or a sequence of lessons. Teachers may first plan a unit of instruction from the progression for a period of several weeks with specified outcomes for learning. These outcomes will

Figure 4.2   The Drivers of Formative Assessment

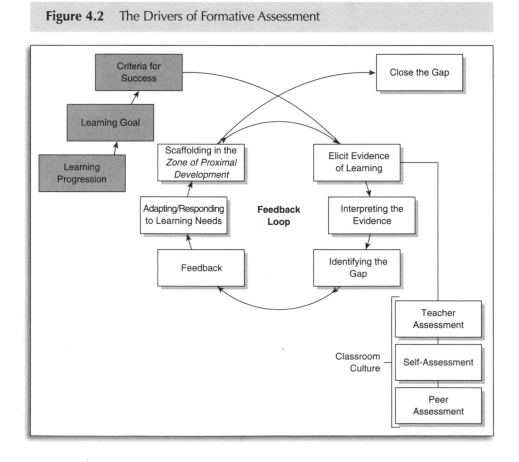

need to be broken down into subgoals for shorter periods of time, such as a lesson or a week's lessons. The subgoals will make clear what the students will learn during the lesson(s). For example, from their measurement and number progression, the New York teachers identified the learning goals:

- Understand that a unit of measure is proportional to its whole (e.g., a centimeter is a proportion of a meter).
- Understand any unit of measure can be divided into any number of equal subunits.

And their success criteria, the indications that the teachers and their students would use to check learning against were:

- Compare parts of a whole to identify the fractional relationship.
- On a number line from 0–12, accurately determine the fractional parts from $\frac{1}{2}$ of the segment to $\frac{1}{12}$ of the segment.
- Explain why on a number line whole numbers increase from left to right but fraction denominators decrease from left to right.

In the next section, we are going to see several examples of learning goals and success criteria teachers have identified for their lesson; a lesson can span one period or several periods. Before the teachers decided on any learning experiences or any formative assessment strategies to use in the lesson, they first specified the learning goals and the success criteria. Remember, the learning goal specifies the learning that is intended, while the success criteria indicate how a student can demonstrate the learning. Taken together, the learning goal and success criteria enable both teacher and students to develop a conception of the goal being aimed for. When reading these, bear in mind that they are all actual examples of efforts by teachers to make formative assessment work. They are not intended as definitive examples or counsels of perfection! Rather, they provide us with opportunities to see how others have tackled the issues of implementation, and to give us encouragement, guidance, and points of debate.

IDENTIFYING LEARNING GOALS AND SUCCESS CRITERIA

Figure 4.3 shows the learning goals and success criteria that Sharon Pernisi, a teacher from Syracuse City School District, identified for a sixth-grade mathematics lesson.

Figure 4.3 Sharon's Learning Goals and Success Criteria

Big Idea: Identify and plot points in all four quadrants.	
Learning Goals	*Success Criteria*
Understand the structure of a coordinate grid.	Talk and write about accurately plotting points on a coordinate grid using correct vocabulary.
Relate the procedure of plotting points to the structure of a coordinate grid.	Accurately plot and label points in each quadrant on a coordinate grid.
	Create a rule about coordinates for each quadrant.

Prior to identifying these goals, Sharon and her colleagues developed a progression of what students needed to learn to be able to meet the state standard "Identify and plot points in all four quadrants." The goals in Figure 4.3 express the learning she wants to take place in her classroom during two or three periods as a result of the experiences she provides for her students. The success criteria are the indicators that she and the students can use to check their learning against as they work to meet the learning goals. Notice that the success criteria are written in a way her students can understand.

In Figure 4.4, we can see how a high school science teacher, Colleen Reese, from Iowa, took a big idea from the state's core curriculum and developed learning goals and success criteria. Colleen has identified an important subgoal of the big idea and then specified what students would be doing or saying if they were on the way to meeting the goal.

Figure 4.4 Colleen's Learning Goals and Success Criteria

Big Idea: There is a system containing different components that interact to influence or create climate over time.	
Learning Goal	*Success Criteria*
Develop the skills to analyze paleoclimatological evidence to reveal historical patterns of warming and cooling of the earth.	Explain the best ways to analyze large data sets for trends.
	Demonstrate and explain how to manipulate data (combining, averaging, finding % change) and accurately graph the results of the analysis.
	Accurately identify patterns of warming and cooling trends.
	Justify conclusions by articulating evidence for basis of conclusion.

From the language arts area, Figure 4.5 shows the reading learning goal and success criteria that Alejandra Santini from Los Angeles identified and explained to her first-grade students before they read aloud. The students knew what to be thinking about while they were reading. They had a conception of the goal being aimed for.

Figure 4.5   Alejandra's Learning Goal and Success Criteria

Reading Goal	Success Criteria
Use reading strategies together to make meaning while you are reading aloud.	Use what you know about sounds and symbols.
	Use what you know about language.
	Use what you already know about the topic.
	Use context cues.
	Remember to self-correct.

When Judy Knowles, a middle school teacher from Los Angeles, planned the learning goal and success criteria for a lesson focused on reading and responding to literature, this is what she wrote:

Figure 4.6   Judy's Learning Goal and Success Criteria

Big Idea: Read and respond to works of literature.	
Learning Goal	Success Criteria
Write a critical analysis of the *Old Man and the Sea.*	Present a judgment that is interpretive, analytic, or evaluative.
	Support your judgment through references to the text, other works, and other authors.

Once again, the criteria for success are clear indications to the student about what is required to meet the specified learning goal. They are also clear indications to Judy about what she is looking for, as well. In this process, Judy and her students will have a shared means of comparing actual performance with the goal (Sadler, 1989).

In Figure 4.7, we can see the goal and success criteria that guided Jessica Gogerty's physics lesson for her ninth-grade students. Jessica is a teacher in Iowa, and the overall big idea was drawn from Iowa's Core Curriculum. Her learning goal is connected to the big idea, and the success criteria indicate what it means to make progress to meet the goal.

Figure 4.7 Jessica's Learning Goal and Success Criteria

Big Idea: Use data to draw conclusions.	
Learning Goal	*Success Criteria*
Understand the relationships between variables that affect standing waves in strings.	Be able to measure cyclical motion using frequency.
	Accurately differentiate between resonating and vibrating in strings.
	Design tests for variables that affect fundamental frequency of strings and draw conclusions.

Up till now, we have seen examples from science, math, and language arts teachers. However, formative assessment is not specific to these subjects. Formative assessment is a process that is used in all subject areas. For example, in Figures 4.8 and 4.9, we can see the learning goals and success criteria an art teacher and a Spanish teacher identified for their lesson. Deb Jensen, also from Iowa, specified the learning goals and success criteria for her third-grade students' art lessons. We can see these in Figure 4.8.

Figure 4.8 Deb's Learning Goals and Success Criteria

Big Idea: Colors have value and intensity.	
Learning Goals	*Success Criteria*
Understand how colors are affected by adding black and white to create shades and tints.	Create different tints and shades of the same color and explain why the color changes.
Understand how artists use tints and shades to create various effects in their work.	Explain how artists have created effects using tints and shades in artwork.
Use accurate vocabulary.	When you are explaining why color changes of how an artist used tints and shades, include accurate vocabulary in your explanation.

Deb clearly specifies the indicators she and her students will use to check on their learning.

Figure 4.9 shows the planning Karissa Guillén did for her middle school Spanish lesson.

Figure 4.9   Karissa's Learning Goals and Success Criteria

Big Idea: Effectively communicating in the target language includes introductions, descriptions, and talking about likes and dislikes.	
Learning Goal	*Success Criteria*
Use infinitive verbs and present tense, in simple declarative sentences, to talk about likes and dislikes.	Identify the infinitive form of verbs.
	Explain the similarities and differences between the Spanish grammar of likes/dislikes to English.
	Use infinitive verbs and grammar structures to form sentences about your likes/dislikes.

We can see how Karissa has developed a conception of what it means to reach the learning goal in the way she has identified the criteria for success.

The next example shows how Gabriela Cardenas has drawn from two subject areas, science and the visual arts, and integrated learning goals for her lesson.

Figure 4.10   Gabriela's Learning Goals and Success Criteria

Big Ideas: Adaptations in physical structure or behavior may improve an organism's chance for survival (Science). Respond to sensory information through the language and skills unique to the Visual Arts.	
Learning Goal	*Success Criteria*
Use what we have learned about line in your observational drawings of cacti.	Make detailed observation of cacti. Use lines of different thickness and direction to show the features of the cacti.
Use vocabulary from the visual arts and science and use in sentence structures to describe your observations of the features of the desert plants.	Describe what you observe in complete sentences. Use the science vocabulary and art vocabulary to talk about your drawing.
Understand the features of desert plants and how they are adapted to their environment.	Make some hypotheses about why cacti can live in the desert. Identify the features of plants that lead to your hypothesis.

Gabriela has integrated the learning goals and success criteria for science and art into a single experience of observational drawing. Notice, too, that Gabriela is very specific about the language she wants the students to produce. This is because all her students are English learners, and in her school English language development takes place in the content areas.

In our final example of learning goals and success criteria, we see how Tonya Urbatsch and Sherry Scott from Iowa identified their learning goals and success criteria. Figure 4.11 shows the level of detail that went into their planning, including specifying the subconcepts, the prerequisite knowledge needed, the learning goals and success criteria, and the question that would drive the students' investigation.

Figure 4.11   Tonya and Sherry's Learning Goals and Success Criteria

Title: Shoelaces Grade 8 or 9 (Two class periods)	
Essential Concept(s)	1. Statistics and Probability: Analyze and summarize data sets, including initial analysis of variability. 2. Algebra: Use linear functions, and understanding of the slope of a line and constant rate of change, to analyze situations and solve problems.
Subconcept(s)	• Informally determine a line of best fit for a scatterplot to make predictions and estimates. • Use linear functions, and understanding of the slope of a line and constant rate of change to analyze situations and solve problems.
Prerequisite Knowledge	• Coordinate Graphing • Slope • Linear Equations
Learning Goal	Understand that • Data can be represented with a linear model. • The linear model gives the power of prediction. • The linear model has limitations.
Success Criteria	I can 1. Organize data and identify patterns in the data. 2. Explain where to draw a line that would be a representation of the relationship and explain why it is a good representation. 3. Explain the limitations of a linear model. 4. Write an equation to represent the line and explain how the parts of the equation were found. 5. Use the line to predict relationships beyond the data provided. 6. Explain how a mathematical model can be used to make predictions.
Focus Question	How can a mathematical model help describe the relationship between the eyelets on a pair of shoes and the length of the laces?

Tonya and Sherry have identified quite a number of success criteria for this problem-based math lesson. Not wanting to overwhelm their students, they decided they would not share all the criteria with them from the outset of the lesson, but instead would introduce them incrementally, as each stage of the lesson progressed.

In each of the examples of learning goals and success criteria, we can see that teachers have identified what *learning* they intend to occur during a lesson. Remember, a lesson can span several periods. Notice the teachers have not yet identified what the students are going to *do* to promote that learning. They will plan the learning opportunities only after the learning goal and success criteria are specified. *Central to the teachers' approach here is the idea that student activities in the course of a lesson are designed to engage students in the learning that will enable them to meet the success criteria, and ultimately, the learning goal.*

Also notice that the success criteria are indications of what it means to reach the learning goal. Teachers have thought carefully about how they will know—what they will see and hear—to indicate that students are making progress toward meeting the goal. They have also thought about how they will express the success criteria to students so that they can use them as checks on their learning while they are engaged in learning experiences. All the teachers have met Sadler's condition of possessing "a concept of the *standard* (or goal, or reference level) being aimed for" (p. 121).

At the beginning of this section, we observed that these examples are illustrations of teachers' efforts to develop clarity about learning goals and success criteria. They are surely not the end of the story! In particular, teachers will have to continue to detail and sharpen their criteria of what successful performances consist of. Ideally, this will be an ongoing and collaborative process, engaging teachers and administrators at all levels of the school.

REVISING LEARNING GOALS AND SUCCESS CRITERIA

Learning goals and success criteria are not fixed and can change as a result of implementing the lesson. For example, Melanie Cifonelli, from Syracuse City School District, wanted to teach her eighth-grade math students the concept of slope. In Figure 4.12, we can see her original learning goals and success criteria for her lesson.

Figure 4.12 Melanie's Learning Goals and Success Criteria

Learning Goals	Success Criteria
Understand the concept of slope	Describe in writing and using pictures what I believe slope is using new vocabulary
Understand that there are different types of slopes and these slopes look different on a graph and in an equation	Decide and justify what type of slope I am making for each graph

Melanie wasn't entirely satisfied with the goal she had identified, and in an e-mail exchange with her colleagues, Melanie commented about the lesson goals:

I hesitated to list slope as a rate in the learning goal, because I want students to come to that understanding through investigation instead of my telling the students that I want you to understand slope as a rate, and then I have given them what slope is before they have investigated it.

Her colleague, Sharon, responded:

I have struggled with the "discovery" piece in the past, too. I wonder if using words like "relate" or "connect" in your learning goal with regard to slope and rate would help? That way, students are aware they are looking for a relationship from the onset of the lesson, but they still need to discover the nature of that relationship through inquiry.

Melanie replied:

Sharon, you are a Learning Goal writing QUEEN! I went ahead today and focused students on what the connection is between slope and rate. The lesson felt much more focused, and students were still working on the exploration. Also, as I went around and asked students what they thought the connection was between slope and rate, they were telling me what was happening in terms of time and distance (like we were covering more distance in less time . . . the faster we went, the steeper the slope). Really excellent explanations! Collaboration is key to this whole process.

This exchange illustrates that learning goals and success criteria can be revised after the lesson implementation if the teacher feels, as in Melanie's case, they were not expressing what she wanted them to learn, and the lesson had not developed in the way she hoped. It also illustrates the importance of collaboration with colleagues. Sharing ideas and getting feedback helped Melanie frame the lesson goals in a more precise way for what she wanted to accomplish. Sharon had already struggled with the idea of identifying learning goals in ways that permitted investigative approaches, and she was able to share what she had learned to benefit Melanie.

COMMUNICATING LEARNING GOALS AND SUCCESS CRITERIA TO STUDENTS

An important point about the process of formative assessment is that from the outset of the lesson, teachers communicate the goal and criteria to their students. Why?

Learning goals focus students' attention on what it is they are to learn, as opposed to the task they are to complete. They enable students to know what they are learning and why, and thus to become active participants in learning rather than passive recipients. Students know what the focus of their learning is while they are engaged in the task, they possess a concept of the goal being aimed for, and they are able to monitor how their learning is progressing in relation to the criteria *during* learning. We'll be looking at the idea of students' self-monitoring in more detail in Chapter 6.

In addition to developing new skills and understandings, students who are focused on learning goals develop a greater sense of intrinsic motivation (Ames, 1992; Ames & Archer, 1988). Students motivated by learning goals "apply effort in acquiring new skills, seek to understand what is involved rather than just committing information to memory, persist in the face of difficulties and generally try to increase their competence" (Harlen, 2007, p. 65). This accords with Carol Dweck's work on self-theories of motivation (Dweck, 1999). She proposes that there are two views of intelligence: an entity view and an incremental view. People who have an entity view consider intelligence or ability to be fixed and stable. Students with an entity view of intelligence are oriented to performance goals. They want to perform better than others, and they limit themselves to tasks they can succeed in so as to avoid failure. An entity view can also lead to "learned helplessness"— students may believe that they are not smart enough to learn and perform well, and therefore give up easily.

People who have an incremental view of intelligence believe intelligence or ability can be changed. Students with this view of intelligence are focused on learning and mastery as opposed to performance goals. They are interested in learning and meeting challenges and believe that effort, engagement in learning, and strategy development can lead to increased intelligence. They are not concerned about failure, as are performance-oriented students, but instead regard errors as new sources of learning. They view these errors as opportunities to revise learning strategies so as to be successful. Teachers must be in the business of promoting this kind of mastery orientation, rather than a performance-orientation.

Teachers need to encourage students "to value learning over the appearance of smartness, to relish challenge and effort, and to use errors as routes to mastery" (Dweck, 1999, p. 4). An essential component in this engagement is to ensure a focus on learning goals and success criteria, and make sure that students understand them and regard them as achievable. Only when students understand the goal and the success criteria, and regard them as achievable and worth learning, will students make the commitment to the goal.

It is essential to make sure that the goal and success criteria are understandable. This means communicating them to students in language appropriate to the students' level. In addition to specifying the success criteria, teachers can also provide exemplars of what the success criteria look like in practice. In this regard, Mr. Gibson in Chapter 2 shared exemplars of the multi-genres essay with his students so they could develop a conception of what the success criteria meant before they embarked on their own writing. To develop students' conception of what it meant to analyze data sets for trends, Colleen Reese, the high school science teacher, shared examples of previous analyses, and she discussed with the students which ones they thought were the most effective and why. Another way to develop a conception of the goal and success criteria is for teachers to draw attention to the criteria while teaching. For example, one of the instructional strategies Sharon Pernisi (see Figure 4.3) used in her lesson was to place a very large coordinate plane on the floor. The students sat around the plane. Sharon gave individual students ordered pairs and asked them to stand on the exact point on the coordinate plane to show the ordered pair. They then explained to their classmates why they were standing in the particular place they had selected. While they were engaged in this activity, Sharon referred back to the success criterion, "I can talk and write about plotting points on a coordinate grid using correct vocabulary," to help them understand what the criteria meant. When the students were subsequently engaged in their group tasks, they had a clear idea of the success criteria they were aiming to meet.

Whatever the means, the more teachers can help students develop the conception of what is being aimed for in learning, the more the students can actively participate in the process of formative assessment.

The practices described in the chapter amount to a kind of compass that helps teachers and students stay on track. In a brilliant observation about school experience, Mary Alice White likened going to school to life onboard a ship. A child, she observed, "only knows he is going to school. Very quickly, the daily life onboard ship becomes all important. The daily chores, the demands, the inspections, become the reality, not the voyage, nor the destination" (White, 1971). The formulation of clear learning goals and success criteria are essential to maintain everyone's focus on the voyage and the destination, and not the chores.

In the following chapter, we move to the next step in formative assessment once the learning goals and success criteria have been established—identifying the formative assessment strategies that will help teachers and their students "compare the actual level of performance" with the goal.

SUMMING UP

- Learning progressions describe a pathway of learning for students and teachers.
- Explicit learning progressions can assist teachers to plan instruction and formative assessment.
- Learning goals and success criteria drive the process of formative assessment.
- Success criteria are checks on learning that students can use as they monitor their own learning.
- Learning goals and success criteria need to be communicated to students in language they can understand.

REFLECTION QUESTIONS

1. How does what you currently do in your classroom compare with the ideas presented in this chapter?

2. What is your current instructional and assessment planning process? Are you clear about what it is that you want your students to learn and how you will know if they are moving forward?

3. Which of the examples of teacher practice in this chapter do you think are strong? Which examples do you think could be improved? How would you improve them?

4. Based on what you have read, what would you like to work on? What support will you need?

5

Formative Feedback for Teaching

In previous chapters, we emphasized the centrality of feedback for effective formative assessment. Formative assessment provides feedback to teachers from the evidence they collect in the course of teaching and learning. This feedback is something they feed forward into their instruction to improve student learning. This is formative feedback for teaching.

The other recipients of feedback are the students. Student feedback comes from their own internal monitoring during learning, or externally from their teachers. This is formative feedback for learning.

In this chapter, we are going to focus on formative feedback for teaching and address formative feedback for learning in the next chapter.

GENERATING THE EVIDENCE

Formative assessment for teaching must answer the following questions:

- Where is the student going?
- Where is the student now?
- Where to next?

In the previous chapter, we saw that the first job in formative assessment is to define the learning goals and the success criteria for the lesson or lessons—where is the student going? Once these are in place, as you can see from Figure 5.1, the teacher's next step is to plan the formative assessment strategies that will elicit the evidence needed to provide feedback for learning—where is the student now? This feedback, in turn, will shape what the teacher will do next to help the student to close the gap between his or her current learning status and the learning goals—where to next?

QUALITY FEEDBACK FOR TEACHING

Recall from Chapter 2, there is no one single way to "do" formative assessment.

In this chapter, we will see a range of evidence-gathering strategies from questioning, to representations, to exit cards at the end of the lesson. In Chapter 3, we learned about the importance of validity and reliability as features of assessment practice. While the issues of validity and reliability (American Educational Research Association, American Psychological Association, & National Council on Measurement in Education, 1999) do not seamlessly transfer to the formative assessment context, teachers need to be aware that the evidence generated from formative strategies must be of sufficient quality to enable them to understand where the learner is in relation to the success criteria and the learning goal. To assure quality evidence,

Figure 5.1 Formative Feedback

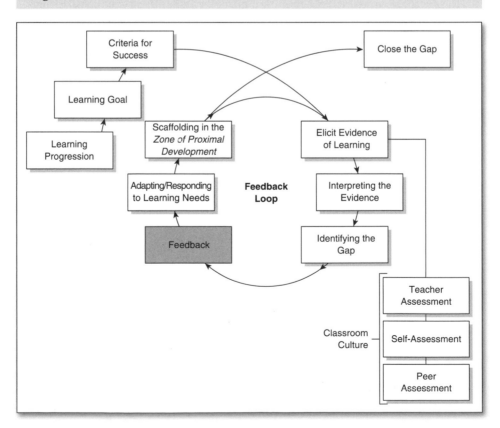

there are a number of factors to bear in mind when selecting formative assessment strategies[1]:

1. The strategies need to be aligned to the learning goal and the success criteria. Remember, the whole point of the formative assessment evidence is to check student learning to make sure it is on the right track to meet the success criteria and the learning goal, and if it isn't, to make adjustments to teaching and learning. Alignment is paramount for this.

2. Because the purpose of formative assessment is to "form" new learning, either by continuing with the planned lesson or by making changes in light of evidence, formative assessment strategies must provide sufficiently detailed evidence to be able to take action.

3. There will be a range of levels of understanding or skill in any classroom, so the strategies must take account of that and permit students of all levels to show where they are in their learning.

4. It is important to use more than one strategy to elicit evidence of how well students are meeting the success criteria, for example, posing a range of questions that invite explanations, a representation to illustrate level of understanding, and a discussion among peers. Not only will a number of different strategies provide teachers with multiple ways to check on learning, but they will also give students the opportunity to show what they understand or can do in a variety of forms.

Now let's look at how the teachers we saw in Chapter 4 generated evidence to provide them with feedback for teaching. Remember, these examples are for encouragement, guidance, and points of debate, and are not offered as counsels of perfection.

REVISITING THE TEACHERS

Figure 5.2 contains the formative assessment strategies Sharon Pernisi included in the coordinate graphing lesson for her sixth-grade students. Notice that the strategies are aligned to the learning goal and success criteria (SC). She has also provided different ways for students to show where they are in their learning, and she has placed the assessment strategies at strategic points in the lesson to keep track of how student learning is developing.

---

1. Thanks to Joan Herman and Ellen Osmundson for their insights about factors for quality formative assessment.

Figure 5.2 Sharon's Formative Assessment Strategies

Start of Lesson	Middle of Lesson	End of Lesson
Vocabulary check: Whip Around What comes to mind when you think of coordinate graphing?	Large group (SC2): Students walk coordinates and label each location on large floor graph.	Cooperative groups (SC 3): Generalize quadrant location for set of coordinates verbally and in writing.
Look for target vocab: Origin, x-axis, y-axis, coordinates, quadrant.	Describe process verbally using vocabulary (SC1).	Chart to create rules for each quadrant and gallery walk (SC 3).
Students write key words on white boards to share, then call on some to explain.	Plot and label points in four quadrants individually—"Design Robertsville" (SC1, 2).	Reflection—self-assessment of SC.

Sharon also thought carefully about the questions she would use throughout her lesson, both to scaffold learning and to elicit evidence. Notice, too, that these questions are focused and open ended, enabling her to capture the different levels of thinking among her students.

Sharon's Questions

- *Start of Lesson:* Are we in agreement with these definitions? How might we make definitions more clear? Are any big ideas missing? How might some of these terms go together?
- *Middle of Lesson:* Where should you start? How would you label this point? Are we in agreement? Tell me your thinking. How do you know you've plotted this point correctly?
- *End of Lesson:* What are you noticing about all the coordinates in this quadrant? How are they alike? How might you develop a rule for all the coordinates in this quadrant? How might you organize the coordinates in quadrant 1 so you can analyze them? (a list, chart, table . . .)

Sharon also makes some notes of what she would be looking out for during the lesson so that she is prepared for any adjustments she needs to make based on student responses.

Sharon's Notes

- Learning goal and success criteria will be shared after initial vocabulary activity.
- Whip around—watch for target vocabulary—if it does not come out of the whip around, more direct vocab. instruction may be needed before moving on.
- Some students may not be conceptually ready to make generalization—they may need more experience with the structure (concrete) of the grid.

Jessica Gogerty made the plan in Figure 5.3 for how she would gather evidence of learning her high school physics lesson.

Figure 5.3 Jessica's Formative Assessment Strategies

Big Idea: Use data to draw conclusions.

Learning Goal	Success Criteria	Formative Assessment Strategies
Describe variables that affect standing waves in strings.	Be able to measure cyclical motion using frequency.	Informal skills test using lab equipment to measure frequency. Teacher observes student skills with equipment. Make brief clipboard notes to review later.
	Differentiate between resonating and vibrating in strings.	*Question:* What would higher frequency look like in the string? *Discussion:* When is the vibrating string resonating? Demo at 1st, 2nd, 3rd harmony and between harmonic frequencies. How will you know when it is resonating?
	Brainstorm variables that affect fundamental frequency of strings.	*Demo:* How do I change the note a guitar will play? How is the string different when it plays a different note?
	Design tests for those variables.	*Question:* How will you control variables? Test one variable with equipment. Check student designs for controlling variables and testing intended variable.
	Draw conclusions from test data.	Write conclusion statement that is supported by data.

Her strategies are aligned to the learning goal and success criteria. Her questions are also focused and open ended so that she can capture the range of understanding in her class. She has also thought about the kind of information her strategies will yield.

In Figure 5.4, we can see the strategies Colleen Reese, the high school science teacher, included in her lesson on paleoclimatological evidence.

Figure 5.4 Colleen's Formative Assessment Strategies

Big Idea: There is a system containing different components that interact to influence or create climate over time.

Learning Goal	Success Criteria	Formative Assessment Strategies
Develop the skills to analyze paleo-climatological evidence to reveal historical patterns of warming and cooling on the earth.	Explain the best way to analyze data sets for trends. Demonstrate and explain how to manipulate data (combining, averaging, finding % change) and accurately graph the results of the analysis.	*Questioning:* Examples of analysis from previous years' students. Is this a good way to analyze the data for trends? If so, why? If not, why not? Paired work to provide explanations. *Observation and questioning:* Individual work on graphing. Why have you chosen to manipulate the data in *X* way? What would happen if you . . . ? *Exit card:* How did your learning go today? Any problems with graphing or analyzing data? *Observation of discussion:* Small groups, individuals present graphs of the analysis to peers and explain logic of analysis. Peers provide feedback.
	Accurately identify patterns of warming and cooling trends. Draw conclusions from patterns. Justify conclusions using relevant data.	*Individual written explanations:* What patterns have you observed in the data? Justify your conclusions with evidence.

All the assessment strategies Colleen planned are aligned to the success criteria, and there are several strategies for each criterion. She selected a range of strategies including individual work, which she would observe and ask students questions to help her understand their thinking, peer feedback, and individual written work. While students can learn from their peers' feedback, teachers can learn about student thinking from the feedback the peers provide to their classmates. Students reveal quite a lot about their own understanding when they have to consider someone else's work and provide comments related to the success criteria. Colleen also gets information about student learning when she asks them to complete an exit card at the end of the lesson. The students leave these cards with her so that she can quickly review them before the next lesson to see what problems, if any, the students are experiencing and would like help with.

In the next example, we see the strategies Deb Jansen planned for her third-grade art lessons.

Figure 5.5   Deb's Formative Assessment Strategies

Big Idea: Colors have value and intensity.		
Learning Goals	*Success Criteria*	*Formative Assessment Strategies*
Understand how colors are affected by adding black and white to create shades and tints.	Create different tints and shades of the same color and explain why the color changes.	*Entrance ticket:* Describe what impact you expect adding black to blue, yellow, and red will have. Describe what impact you expect adding white will have. Review responses as students begin experimenting. *Individual experimentation:* Paint colors to create shades and tints. *Questioning:* What did you do to make this shade/tint? What do you think would happen if you added white to this color? Why? What do you think would happen if you added black? Why?
Understand how artists use tints and shades to create various effects in their work.	Explain how artists have used tints and shades in their work.	In small groups, discuss three pictures from different artists. How has the artist used tints and shades? What kind of effects have they created? Teacher observation of discussions—intervene to scaffold. Group presentations to the class—peer feedback.
Use accurate vocabulary.	When you are explaining why color changes, or how an artist used tints and shades, include accurate vocabulary in your explanation.	Listen for vocabulary use in all of the above.

Once again, we see that Deb, too, has closely aligned the formative assessment strategies with the learning goal and success criteria. She identified a series of questions to probe students' understanding of how tints and shades are created while they are experimenting with color, and she included opportunities to assess learning through observations of group discussions and peer feedback. Notice that her questions are broad enough to capture the range of knowledge and understanding among the class.

When Alejandra Santini, from Para Los Niños Charter School in Los Angeles, planned her reading assessment strategies (see Figure 5.6), she also aligned them to the success criteria. The strategies included listening, observation, and recording, and also student self-assessment. Asking her students to think about their own reading helped Alejandra understand if they were aware of the strategies they had been learning about and how effective they thought they were in using them. Not only does this assessment strategy provide Alejandra with information about the students' thinking, but it also gives the students the opportunity to develop metacognitive skills—thinking about thinking—which as we will learn in Chapter 6 is a hallmark of effective learning.

Figure 5.6   Alejandra's Formative Assessment Strategies

Reading Goal	Success Criteria	Formative Assessment Strategies
Use reading strategies together to make meaning while you are reading aloud.	Use what you know about sounds and symbols.	Listen to individual read aloud, note strategies used, how often, how effectively.
	Use what you know about language.	Note any strategies not used.
	Use what you already know about the topic.	At end of reading, ask student what strategies he or she was using.
	Use context cues.	
	Remember to self-correct.	Ask how well the student thought he or she was using them.

In the example, Judy Knowles, a middle school writing teacher, shows the process she used to assess student writing as they draft a response to literature.

Figure 5.7   Judy's Formative Assessment Strategies

Big Idea: Read and respond to works of literature.		
Learning Goal	*Success Criteria*	*Formative Assessment Strategies*
Write a critical analysis of the *Old Man and the Sea*.	Present a judgment that is interpretive, analytic, or evaluative. Support your judgment through references to the text, other works, and other authors.	First draft: Partner peer review and feedback. Note to teacher about what sections they would like to discuss. Second draft: Student highlights improvements, then peer review and feedback. Teacher review of feedback and add comment(s). Final draft.

Among the several formative assessment strategies used here is teacher review of the feedback a partner has given. This will give the teacher insights into how the student partners are thinking about their own judgments, and the support they provide for them. In addition, the student self-assessment will provide insights into areas of difficulty they have, or help they need. The strategies are aligned to the learning goal and success criteria. They will capture the range of levels of learning among the students, and they will also provide the teacher with information that can be used to improve the students' work.

Figure 5.8 shows the strategies Karissa Guillén selected to obtain information about the language learning of her students.

Figure 5.8   Karissa's Formative Assessment Strategies

Big Idea: Effectively communicating in the target language includes introductions, descriptions, and talking about likes and dislikes.		
Learning Goal	*Success Criteria*	*Formative Assessment Strategies*
Use infinitive verbs and present tense, in simple declarative sentences, to talk about likes and dislikes.	I will identify the infinitive form of verbs.	*Observation:* Teacher gives students a verb and students act it out (teacher watches to see who can act them out).

(Continued)

Figure 5.8 (Continued)

Learning Goal	Success Criteria	Formative Assessment Strategies
	I will explain the similarities and differences between the Spanish grammar of likes or dislikes to English.	*Questioning:* Ask students to explain how to form sentences about likes and dislikes—how is the structure different from English? Students produce sentences orally.
	I will use infinitive verbs and grammar structures to form sentences about my likes/dislikes.	*Writing performance:* Students will write sentences about what they like to do and what they do not like to do.

Karissa's formative assessment strategies are varied, they are aligned to the learning goal and success criteria, and they will provide her with the range of learning levels in her classroom.

In the next example, we see how Gabriela Cardenas from Para Los Niños Charter School in downtown Los Angeles has integrated formative assessment strategies for learning goals from two subject areas, science and the visual arts, into her lesson.

Figure 5.9 Gabriela's Formative Assessment Strategies

Big Ideas: Adaptations in physical structure or behavior may improve an organism's chance for survival (Science). Respond to sensory information through the language and skills unique to the Visual Arts.		
Learning Goal(s)	Success Criteria	Formative Assessment Strategies
Use what we have learned about line in your observational drawings of cacti.	I can make detailed observation of cacti. I can use lines of different thickness and direction to show the features of the cacti.	Field trip to cactus garden, individual observational drawings from sensory information—teacher observation of detail and line. Provide feedback to students.

Learning Goal(s)	Success Criteria	Formative Assessment Strategies
Use vocabulary from the visual arts and science and use in sentence structures to describe your observations of the features of the desert plants.	I can describe what I observe in complete sentences. I can use the science vocabulary and art vocabulary to talk about my drawing.	In pairs, before drawing describe to each other what they observe—teacher listens. After observation class discussion for students to share what they have observed. Teacher discussion with the students during drawing, questioning: Tell me about your drawing—what do you see? How do your lines show the texture of the cactus? How have you used line to show the surface of the cactus?
Understand the features of desert plants and how they are adapted to their environment.	I can make some hypotheses about why cacti can live in the desert. I can identify the features of plants that lead to my hypothesis.	In groups, using observational drawing, discuss the features and come up with at least one hypothesis. Groups present to class—peer and teacher feedback. Check on any misconceptions.

Gabriela uses a variety of strategies, from observation, to discussion, to group presentations. Each strategy is designed to provide her with information related to both her science and visual arts goals, as well as the language learning of her English learner students. The strategies are well aligned to her success criteria, and they are sufficiently broad to permit the range of knowledge and skill represented among her students to be expressed and for any misconception related to science understanding to surface.

Tonya Urbatsch and Sherry Scott went one step further than the other teachers. Figure 5.10 shows some of the success criteria and the questions they planned to ask the students during the lesson to elicit evidence of learning. They have also identified likely student responses or actions, and how they would respond to them if they arise in the lesson. Tonya and Sherry have integrated instruction and assessment. Knowing the possible student responses to their questions enables them to be prepared for appropriate instructional action during the lesson.

Figure 5.10 Tonya and Sherry's Formative Assessment Strategies

Success Criteria: Instructional and Formative Assessment Strategies		
Questions	*Possible Student Responses or Actions*	*Possible Teacher Responses*
1. Organize data and identify patterns in the data.		
How are you keeping track of the data you are working with?		Would it help to put them in order? Have you tried a table?
What do you notice about these data?	There are numbers missing. It is not organized. There are duplicates of eyelets with different lengths.	
Describe a pattern in the data.	The lengths generally increase as the number of eyelets gets bigger.	You showed pattern in the table. Could you show it another way like in a graph?
2. Explain where to draw a line that would be a representation of the relationship and explain why it is a good representation.		
How did you decide where to draw the line to represent the data?	The line goes through the data points so that most of the points are on or near the line.	
How does the line you drew help describe the data?		
Is there only one line that is possible?		How would you choose which line is the best?
3. Explain the limitations of a linear model.		
Can you think of a situation in which that line would not be a good representation of the overall relationship?	If the points weren't in a linear pattern.	
What could happen if you connected the first and last points in a data set to get your line? What if the first and last points do not follow the pattern?	Sometimes it would work.	It might be possible to create a line that is not close at all to the points you are trying to describe.

As we noted earlier, and as we have seen from these examples, there is no single way to elicit evidence of learning. So let's consider the range of formative assessment strategies these teachers used.

Questions

How do you know you've plotted this point correctly?

How is the string different when it plays a different note? Why is that?

What are you noticing about all the coordinates in this quadrant?

What terms might go together?

What did you do to make this shade/tint? What do you think would happen if you added white to this color?

How do your lines show the texture of the cactus? How have you used line to show the surface of the cactus?

Can you think of a situation in which that line would not be a good representation of the overall relationship?

Tasks Involving Representation

Make designs to control variables and test the intended variable.

Plot coordinate points and describe the process verbally.

Work in groups to create charts of rules for each quadrant and gallery walk.

Write conclusions backed with data.

Experiment with color.

Provide entrance tickets at the start of the lesson.

Write vocabulary words on white boards.

Draw the surface features of cacti.

Write drafts to express a judgment about a work of literature.

Draw the line to best represent the data.

Observation and Listening

Listen to student read aloud and observe use of reading cues.

Listen to students reflect on which reading strategies they used to make meaning.

Observe students' work individually to analyze data sets for trends (notice that the teacher also added questioning to this strategy to get at deeper levels of student understanding).

Observe student skills with lab equipment.

Listen to student discussions.

Listen to peers provide feedback about explanations of artists' use of shades and tints.

Self-Assessment

Provide exit cards (where students write a response to a prompt from the teacher before they leave the lesson).

Reflect on reading.

Collect notes to the teacher about what students would like to discuss.

In all the examples of the teachers' planning, the strategies were aligned with the success criteria and were designed to give the information the teacher needed to check on learning. The teachers used different strategies for students to show where they were in relation to the learning goal, and the strategies enabled teachers to capture the range of learning in the classroom. The teachers also designed the strategies to be seamlessly integrated with instruction. In fact, in some of the examples, it is difficult to differentiate between what is assessment and what is instruction, which is often the case in formative assessment. As Richard Shavelson and colleagues note, "A good assessment makes a good teaching activity, and a good teaching activity makes a good assessment" (Shavelson, Baxter, & Pine, 1992, p. 22).

CURRICULUM-EMBEDDED ASSESSMENT

Not all formative assessment strategies need to be designed by the teacher. Many curricula include useful assessments that can be used formatively during the course of a lesson or unit—(to be formative, unit assessments need to be given before the end of the unit so that adjustments to learning can be made before it's too late). Some units of instruction place assessments at strategic points so that teachers can make sure students have the prerequisite understanding or skill before moving on to another level of learning.

When selecting curricular assessments, it will be important to decide if they are well aligned to learning goals and success criteria that are the focus of current instruction, and if they can provide the level of detail needed to check on learning. Remember, *all* formative assessment—whether teacher designed or commercially produced—should provide quality evidence that can be used to adapt instruction to the learning needs; in other words, provide feedback for teaching.

TECHNOLOGY TOOLS

Several researchers are currently developing very promising technology-based assessments, particularly in the areas of math and science. They are not curriculum specific, but because they focus on important principles and ideas within the domain, they can be used with any curriculum.

The assessments are built on research-based models of learning and are often designed to highlight misconceptions about a topic. *ASSISTments* (www .assistments.org/) and *Diagnostic Algebra Assessments* (Russell & O'Dwyer, 2009) are two examples of such assessments. In addition to helping teachers identify important misconceptions, they provide feedback to students in the form of instructional scaffolding. The assessments have undergone a rigorous process to establish their technical quality (i.e., validity and reliability), and they have the potential to be very valuable resources for teachers. It's a good idea to keep an eye out for such research-based assessments.

HELPER PRACTICES FOR FORMATIVE ASSESSMENT

In addition to the kinds of formative assessment strategies and tools we have seen in this chapter, teachers can use a range of helper practices. By helper practices, we mean instructional techniques that, while not aligned to any particular success criteria, will support those that are. Many of these helper practices can be used in conjunction with the kind of strategies we have seen above. For example, Shirley Clarke (2005) suggests techniques such as "no hands up." Teachers pose a question, give time for the students to think about it, and then use a randomized technique to identify the student to answer the question (e.g., names on popsicle sticks drawn from a cup). This technique keeps all students engaged because they never know whom the teacher will call on. Clarke also suggests a number of other techniques that can be used with questioning strategies:

- *Increase wait time:* If a question is worth asking, that is, if it is going to prompt thinking as opposed to generate a one-word answer, then students need time to answer it.
- *Paired discussions:* To help students formulate their thinking, give them time to talk in pairs before they are asked to respond.

- *Students quickly jot down thoughts:* Similarly, this helps students think about the answer and gives them a chance to make notes before asking them to respond.

Other helper practices can double up as stand-alone checks on learning. For example, Wiliam (2007) suggests the use of traffic lights as a formative assessment technique. This involves giving students red, yellow, and green cards that they can hold up or place in front of them to indicate their level of understanding in response to a question or other prompts. Although the use of these cards does not give insights into students' thinking, it is an effective way to gain a general sense of whether the students think they understand, nearly understand, or don't understand lesson content.

Jill Fendt, from Syracuse, used an adaptation of this practice with her third-grade students. Using red, green, and yellow cups on their desks, they independently moved the cups around as they were working individually or in groups to indicate when they needed help either from a peer or from the teacher.

Another set of helper strategies, called "all-student response" systems, was identified in Leahy et al. (2005). These approaches work hand in hand with the questions teachers might plan as part of their formative assessment process and enable the teacher to not only get better-quality evidence but to get it from more students. Even the most well-crafted question can only tell a teacher so much if only one student responds. These all-student approaches focus on finding ways for teachers to collect evidence from all students simultaneously in a way that is easy to review. For example, students can write short answers, draw diagrams, or write an equation on a white board and hold it up for teachers to see. Alternatively, with a well-crafted multiple-choice question, a teacher might have students use laminated sets of ABCD cards (Wylie & Ciofalo, 2008), allowing a teacher to skillfully direct a discussion by calling on students to explain various answer choices. Teachers could also use clickers for this process. Both are quick ways for a teacher to estimate levels of student understanding and, if the questions are well designed, to identify specific difficulties or common misconceptions. Exit or entrance tickets are another way to quickly collect information from all students, especially if the question prompt for the ticket is crafted in such a way that a response can be written on an index card. When teachers think about the questions they ask, it is important to consider not just the question itself but also how they will enable students to respond.

PLANNING INSTRUCTION AND ASSESSMENT

Effective formative assessment involves eliciting evidence in systematic ways so teachers have a constant stream of information about how student learning is evolving toward the desired goal. A constant stream is necessary because when assessment evidence is used to inform instructional action, then that action, if effective, will render previous assessment information out of date: Student learning will have progressed and will need to be assessed again so that instruction can be adjusted to keep learning moving forward.

In all the examples we have seen in this chapter, teachers planned their formative assessment strategies at the same time as their instruction. Before the beginning of the lesson, they were clear about what they wanted the students to learn, what tasks they would do to facilitate learning, and how they would gather evidence about progress. Systematic planning of this kind ensures that the teachers are integrating assessment into instruction and are keeping constant track of how learning is developing. In the event that the formative assessment information reveals a misconception or a difficulty in learning, they can make the necessary adjustments during the lesson or make plans to address problem areas in subsequent lessons.

However, planning formative assessment ahead of time does not preclude spontaneous formative assessment arising during the lesson. Spontaneous formative assessment is when teachers get an insight from something the students do or say during the instructional activity, sometimes referred to as a "teachable moment." In this case, the teacher changes the course of instruction in light of evidence there and then, rather than continuing with the planned lesson. For example, Colleen Reese might find that some of her students have misunderstandings about graphing that prevent them from being able to analyze the data in her science lesson, so she would need to clear these up before they could progress. While listening to one of her students read aloud, Alejandra Santini could find the student had problems decoding words with certain diphthongs she had not anticipated and would use this information in subsequent instructional planning. While it is desirable to plan formative assessment opportunities before the lesson, teachers should always be on the alert for valuable information their students can provide during their learning that can inform subsequent instructional action.

WHO IS ASSESSED AND WHEN?

In large-scale assessment (e.g., statewide and districtwide accountability tests), teachers are told what tests to administer, when to administer them, and typically they have to administer them to all students at the same time. These tests gather information about the performance of students in the entire state, district, and school. In formative assessment, it is the teachers who make the decisions about which students to assess, how often to assess them, what strategies they will use to gauge learning, and whether they will assess individual students, groups, or the whole class. There may be particular students in the class, those who are struggling to understand a concept, for example, that the teacher wants to pay close attention to so their learning doesn't go off track. In this case, she will assess the students more frequently than those whose learning is advancing successfully. Of course, she will assess the more successful students too—otherwise how would she know they were successful!—but not as frequently as those about whom she has concerns.

INTERPRETING EVIDENCE

Having gathered the evidence from formative assessment, whether spontaneously or through planned opportunities during the lesson, the next job for the teacher is to interpret what it means in terms of student learning. Recall that Sadler (1989) stressed that the purpose of formative assessment is to identify the gap between a learner's current status in learning and some desired educational goal.

The learning goal and success criteria provide the framework for interpreting the evidence to identify the gap. Teachers have to determine if the student or students have met the criteria, are on the way to meeting the criteria, or are showing problems, misconceptions, or difficulties. To help with interpretation, particularly if it is during the course of the lesson, it is a good idea to identify a possible range of responses that students might make to the formative assessment strategy and decide what pedagogical action will be appropriate to meet the learning needs. With this kind of forward planning, teachers are equipped to respond to the students there and then.

In the instances where students are on track to attain the learning goal, the teacher will be able to continue with the planned instruction to close the gap. However, in the case where students are not on track, teachers will need to make instructional adjustments in response to the evidence to meet the learning needs. Sometimes this will involve gathering more formative assessment evidence—asking deeper, probing questions to find the source of the misconception or difficulty, or implementing more formative assessment strategies to see if the same problem shows up in other forms of evidence.

THE "JUST RIGHT GAP"

Sadler (1989) also stressed that the gap will vary from student to student and spelled out the consequence for pedagogy: "If the gap is perceived as too large by a student, the goal may be unattainable, resulting in a sense of failure and discouragement on the part of the student. Similarly, if the gap is perceived as too small, [students could feel that] closing it might not be worth any individual effort" (p. 130). In the Goldilocks metaphor, then, formative assessment is a process that needs to identify the "just right gap."

In instructional terms, "just right gap" has been conceived of as the zone of proximal development (ZPD). Originating with Vygotsky, the ZPD is defined as the distance between what the child can accomplish during independent problem solving and the level of problem solving that can be accomplished under the guidance of an adult or in collaboration with a more expert peer (Vygotsky, 1978). As the term implies, Vygotsky conceived the ZPD in the context of the broad maturation of the child's developmental structures (Chaiklin, 2005). The teacher's task is to use formative assessment to identify and build on immature but maturing structures and, through collaboration and guidance, to facilitate cognitive growth. In the process, the student internalizes the resources required for solving a particular problem, and they become part of his or her independent developmental achievement.

Mostly, adapting instruction will not involve reteaching. Only if students have learned nothing at all from instruction will reteaching be necessary. And in this case, it won't really be reteaching in the sense of teaching the same thing over. If students didn't "get it" the first time, then a different approach to teaching the concept or skills should be adopted.

The term "scaffolding" characterizes the support that adults give to learners in the ZPD to move them from what they already know to what they can do next (Wood, Bruner, & Ross, 1976). When teachers interpret evidence, they need to identify the next steps in learning that students can take within the ZPD, and to adapt teaching to close the gap between the student's current learning status and the desired learning goal (Shepard, 2005; Torrance & Pryor, 1998).

DIFFERENTIATING INSTRUCTION

In any classroom, students' learning will not proceed uniformly or evenly. One student's "just right gap" will not necessarily be the same as another's. Therefore, scaffolding learning in the ZPD requires differentiated instruction. Clearly it is not practical, nor even desirable, for teachers to engage in one-on-one instruction for each student—interaction among peers is also a strong component of learning. However, to meet the range of learning needs in any classroom, teachers need to allow for different levels and rates of learning.

Strategic questioning in a whole-class lesson can provide scaffolding for a range of learning levels. By asking advanced students more challenging questions, and to explain their thinking, the teacher helps them deepen their thinking and also enables less advanced students to hear explanations of the idea they are trying to grasp. Weaving questions involving incremental levels of challenge into the lesson can help those students who are trying to grasp the idea to build their thinking.

Forming flexible subgroups for instruction is another way to differentiate learning. Teachers can create need groups when the formative assessment evidence shows there are students at similar levels of understanding. Working with these groups, teachers can target their instruction to specific needs. These learning groups are not fixed because, even though the students may have the same learning need in relation to a particular skill or concept, their needs will change and regrouping will be necessary.

The teacher may meet with some subgroups more frequently than others. For example, she might meet with a more advanced group to prompt them to solve real-world problems in a variety of ways, and then leave them to work together, checking with them periodically to discuss what they are doing and keeping them on track to extend their learning. Other groups, however, may need more fine-grained scaffolding on a frequent basis, taking smaller steps to increase their understanding until they meet the learning goal.

Subgroups of students who are at differing levels of understanding can also be assigned collaborative tasks and investigations where they learn with and from each other. This does not mean the teacher relinquishes responsibility for the learning. Careful listening and observation will be needed so that she can intervene at the appropriate moment to scaffold the more advanced thinkers and make sure the less advanced ones are not getting left behind.

Another differentiating strategy involves engaging groups in different learning tasks related to the same concept, but pitched at the range of learning levels represented in the classroom. Students might be learning the same concept or skill, but the tasks will be at differential levels of complexity depending on what the formative assessment evidence reveals about the students' learning.

Working with individuals will also be necessary to differentiate instruction, particularly for those students who are experiencing real problems and for whom whole class teaching or subgroup learning is just not working.

In the end, no one strategy will be the answer. Teachers must use a range of methods to differentiate instruction depending on the learning need at hand, and they need to be flexible and nimble in implementing the methods in the classroom.

BUILDING A REPERTOIRE

Ultimately, success in adapting instruction to meet learning needs requires teachers to build up a repertoire of effective instructional strategies that can be used during the course of the lesson or during the subsequent lesson. A range of problems, difficulties, or misconceptions is likely to arise in any lesson. A useful way to build a repertoire of instructional strategies, and ways to differentiate instruction, is to think before the lesson what kind of problems or misconceptions students might have with the particular concept or skill they are going to learn. For example, when Sharon Pernisi was planning her lesson on the coordinate plane, she identified three possible problems students might have:

- A procedural graphing misconception—(y, x)
- Plot points in spaces rather than intersections
- Count intervals on lines rather than x or y axes

Sharon also planned what she would do in response to these problems if they arose in the lesson. She started the lesson with a tool kit of instructional strategies she could use if needed so as to keep learning moving along effectively.

Similarly, when Melanie Cifonelli planned her lesson on slope, she identified the following two potential problems:

- Slope is just a number in an equation (Many students can identify slope as being "2" in the equation $y = 2x + 1$, but they do not understand that slope is a rate).
- Slope is just how steep a line is.

If she came across these problems in her lesson, she already had ideas about how she would deal with them.

Collaborating with colleagues to plan formative assessment, to identify possible misconceptions and problems that may arise, and then reviewing together how effective both the formative assessment strategy and the instructional response were can be extremely valuable in building up a pedagogical repertoire. Additionally, some curricula, particularly in the areas of math and science, provide embedded assessments to be used formatively. They specify the potential misconceptions students might have and offer suggestions about ways in which teachers might respond to these pedagogically to differentiate learning.

In Chapter 7, we'll look in more detail about how teachers can develop their formative assessment skills, but for now the important point to keep in mind is there will be differences among students in terms of the gap, and teachers need to develop a repertoire of appropriate responses to meet individual and group learning needs.

In this chapter, we saw that when teachers generate quality evidence, interpret the evidence to make decisions about what the next steps in learning should be, and implement instructional strategies to meet the identified learning needs, they are engaged in a process of using formative feedback for teaching. In the next chapter, we are going to look at the process of formative feedback for learning.

> ### SUMMING UP
>
> - Feedback is central to formative assessment.
> - There is no one single way to "do" formative assessment. Evidence of learning can be gathered by using a range of different strategies and tools.
> - Formative assessment strategies need to be aligned to learning goals and success criteria.
> - Formative assessment strategies need to provide sufficiently detailed information to take action.
> - Formative assessment opportunities are planned at the same time as instructional plans are made, but they can also arise spontaneously in the classroom.
> - Because the gap will differ among students, differentiated instruction should be an outcome of formative assessment.

REFLECTION QUESTIONS

1. How often do you use the kind of formative assessment strategies described in this chapter?

2. What new or additional formative assessment strategies can you envision incorporating into your classroom? What support do you think you will need?

3. How much planning for formative assessment do you do before the lesson? Is this something you could do more often? What support do you think you will need?

4. Which of the examples of teacher practice in this chapter do you think are strong? Which examples do you think could be improved? How would you improve them?

6

Formative Feedback for Learning

When effectively provided, feedback is an immensely powerful engine for improving learning. In their recent review of 196 studies reporting 6,972 effect sizes, Hattie and Timperley (2007) report that feedback had an average effect size of 0.79 standard deviations—an effect greater than student prior cognitive ability, socioeconomic background, and reduced class size (p. 83).

In the previous chapter, we focused on formative feedback for teaching—feedback teachers get from assessment evidence, which they use to make adjustments to teaching to keep learning moving forward. In this chapter, we will look at feedback that is provided directly to the learner. Figure 6.1 shows that feedback feeds forward into planning modifications in learning as well as in teaching.

Two definitions of feedback provide our framework for thinking about formative feedback for learning. Feedback is:

. . . information communicated to the learner that is intended to modify his or her thinking or behavior for the purpose of improving learning. (Shute, 2008, p. 154)

. . . information provided by an agent (e.g., teacher, peer, book, parent, self, experience) regarding aspects of one's performance or understanding. (Hattie & Timperley, 2007, p. 81)

As the definitions make clear, feedback about *learning* is provided to the learner with the intended purpose of improving learning and, as indicated in the second definition, feedback can come from a number of sources. In this chapter, we are going to focus on the external feedback students receive from the teacher and peers, and on the internal feedback students receive during a process of self-assessment. First, we'll look at the feedback teachers provide to their students.

TEACHER FEEDBACK

Whatever the source of the feedback in formative assessment, it should focus on helping students answer the same questions that teachers need to answer:

- Where am I going?
- Where am I now?
- Where to next?

Hattie and Timperley (2007) make clear "the answers to these questions enhance learning when there is a discrepancy between what is understood and what is aimed to be understood" (p. 102). This view echoes Sadler's own model, which, citing Ramaprasad (1983), emphasizes that "information

Figure 6.1   Feedback for Learning

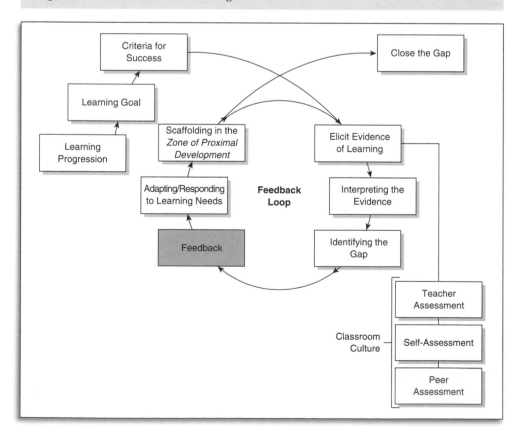

about the gap between actual and reference levels is considered feedback only when it is used to alter the gap" (Sadler, 1989, p. 121). The purpose of feedback to students, then, is to help them identify the gap between where their learning currently stands, and assist them to move forward to close the gap and achieve the desired goals.

TYPES OF TEACHER FEEDBACK

For feedback to be formative it must lead to new learning. Although it is generally accepted that feedback can assist learning, not all types of feedback have positive results. Some examples of the kinds of feedback that can have negative consequences are:

- Feedback that is critical (Baron, 1993)
  o *"This work is very poor. You have not tried hard enough."*

- Feedback that is comparative and indicates a student's standing relative to peers (Black & Wiliam, 1998b; Wiliam, 2007)
  o *"Your understanding of this idea is much weaker than the other students in the class. You will need to redo the work to catch up."*

- Feedback that is vague and lacks specificity (Kluger & DeNisi, 1996)
  o *"Next time, check your calculations."*

- Feedback that is too complex (Kulhavy, White, Topp, Chan, & Adams, 1985)
  o *"You are not paying sufficient attention to the features of narrative in your writing. Revise your work, paying attention to the fact that the features of narrative structures can include orientation, complication and resolution, as well as descriptions of characters and settings. You are emphasizing character and setting without employing a structure that represents the other, important features of narrative. Use all of the features I have indicated above in your next draft."*

- Feedback that draws attention to the student rather than the task (e.g., praise for task performance) (Kluger & DeNisi, 1996)
  o *"You are a good student. I am very pleased with you."*

- Feedback provided in relation to a poorly defined goal (Hattie & Timperley, 2007)
  o *"Write two more paragraphs."*

However, there is ample research about the positive effects of feedback on learning. Key guidelines about the kind of feedback that helps learners improve are listed:

- Feedback should provide information to the student relating to the task or process of learning that fills a gap between what is understood and what is aimed to be understood (Hattie & Timperley, 2007).
- Feedback to students should be about the particular qualities of their work, with advice on what they can do to improve (Bangert-Drowns et al., 1991; Black & Wiliam, 1998a, 1998b).
- Feedback should be specific and clear and be related to learning goals (Hoska, 1993; Song & Keller, 2001).

- Feedback should provide the learner with suggestions, hints, or cues for how to improve rather than correct answers (Bangert-Drowns et al., 1991; Butler, 1987; Kluger & DeNisi, 1996; Narciss & Huth, 2004).
- Feedback should match the student's cognitive needs—not too complex and not too vague (Bangert-Drowns et al., 1991).
- Feedback should include both verification and elaboration. Verification is "the simple judgment of whether the answer is correct and elaboration is the informational aspect of the message, providing relevant clues to guide the learner toward a correct answer" (Shute, 2008, p. 158).
- Feedback should be given after a student has responded to initial instruction. In the case when no learning has occurred, it is better to continue with instruction rather than provide feedback (Hattie & Timperley, 2007)

TIMING OF FEEDBACK

Research has also shown that the timing of the feedback can have both positive and negative consequences. Here are some general guidelines about the timing of feedback:

- It is better to avoid providing feedback to students while they are actively engaged in the task (Corno & Snow, 1986).
- Immediate feedback (i.e., immediately after the student's response) is better for supporting procedural or conceptual knowledge (Dihoff, Brosvic, & Epstein, 2003; Corbett & Anderson, 1989, 2001).
- When a student is learning a new task, immediate feedback is better (Clariana, 1990).
- In the case of more difficult tasks, involving greater amounts of processing, delayed feedback (i.e., feedback after several minutes, hours, or weeks) provides more opportunity for students to process (Clariana, Wagner, & Rohrer-Murphy, 2000).
- Low-achieving students benefit from immediate feedback, particularly when they are learning new concepts or skills they find difficult (Gaynor, 1981; Mason & Bruning, 2001).

While these guidelines can be helpful for teacher decision making about when to give feedback to their students, ultimately, teachers will need to decide when feedback is appropriate for their students, based on the learning goal(s) and their knowledge of students and how they learn best.

FEEDBACK AS INSTRUCTIONAL SCAFFOLDING

In Chapter 5, we looked at the notion of identifying the gap between current levels of learning and desired goals in terms of Vygotsky's concept of the zone of proximal development (ZPD) (Vygotsky, 1978). We also referred to the term "scaffolding" to characterize the support that learners receive in the ZPD to move them from what they already know to what they can do next (Wood, Bruner, & Ross, 1976). When feedback provides models, cues, or hints to support improvements in learning, it is operating as an instructional scaffold. Thus, the distinction between feedback and instruction is blurred: Feedback can be characterized as instruction, and instruction can be characterized as feedback. What is important to remember here is that the feedback and instruction should be targeted within a student's ZPD so that it can help students take the next steps to develop understanding or skills or effective learning strategies.

FEEDBACK AND SELF-REGULATION

Effective learning involves self-regulation. Self-regulated learners monitor their learning against learning goals, they apply learning strategies and tactics when engaged in tasks, and they make adaptations to their strategies and tactics when they judge the need to do so to make progress (Butler & Winne, 1995; Paris & Winograd, 2003; Zimmerman, 2000). Feedback can support self-regulation if it focuses on helping students develop strategy knowledge, the strategies that are most effective in particular domains. Examples include drawing a diagram to solve a mathematical problem, or doing more research to analyze historical events, or re-reading a text to make the meaning clearer. Later in this chapter, we will examine self-assessment as part of self-regulation. But for now, recognize that in providing feedback teachers need to help students build their repertoire of learning strategies and tactics, which they can employ in various learning domains.

EXAMPLES OF TEACHER FEEDBACK

In this section, we are going to look at several examples of feedback and examine each one in relation to the criteria laid out earlier in the chapter.

Example 1

In a sixth-grade science class, students were learning how to design a fair test. The criteria for success provided to the students at the start of the lesson were:

- Be specific about what you want to measure.
- Identify the key variable and factors that you want to hold constant.
- Show a plan to conduct the test.

One student specified that he was going to measure the time it takes a parachute to fall to the ground. He noted in his design that he would change the size of the parachute, but keep the weight and shape of the parachute the same, and the length and thickness of the parachute strings the same. After the student had completed the design, the teacher reviewed it with him and gave this feedback:

> Your design shows that you are clear about what you want to measure, and you have listed four factors that should remain constant in your test and one that will change.
>
> For your test to be fair, there is one other factor that must remain constant. You are planning to measure the time parachutes of different sizes take fall to the ground. With this in mind, can you review your plan and think about what else needs to be constant? I'll be back in a few moments to hear your ideas.

The student reviewed his plan and realized that the height from which the parachute is dropped needs to be constant.

When the teacher returned to check on his thinking she provided this feedback:

> You have planned your fair test in general terms. Now think about how you would conduct your test in a systematic way so that you can draw conclusions from your test. I suggest you review some of the examples of fair tests we looked at from last year's students to help you think about how you will conduct your measurements and record your data in systematic ways so that you can compare your results.

What are the characteristics of this feedback that correspond to the criteria?

- The teacher verified what was correct and elaborated on what need to be done to improve.
- The feedback related to the learning goal and the success criteria.
- The teacher scaffolded learning with the feedback, providing guidance in small increments as the student worked through the task.
- The feedback matched the cognitive demand and was clear and specific.
- The teacher gave the student information to fill the gap between current learning and desired goals.
- The feedback supports self-regulation by giving the students hints he could use to take the next step in his design.

Example 2

In a ninth-grade classroom, students were learning about slope and were given tasks that required students to answer the question, "What is the slope of the line graphed here?" As the teacher circulated among the students to observe their work, this is the feedback she gave to one of the students:

> Remember we talked about slope as the change in y divided by the change in x from point A to point B. See if you can find the change in y from point A to B. I'll be back to check in a few minutes.

This feedback:

- Provided a scaffold for the student—"remember we talked about . . ."
- Provided a hint for how to move forward
- Matched the student's cognitive level
- Supported self-regulation

Example 3

In this example, a first-grader is reading aloud to the teacher. Before beginning to read, the teacher reminds the student to think about the reading strategies they have been working on in her reading group. This is how the student reads:

Text: Fish swim in the sea.

Student (reading very slowly):   Fish. . . . swim . . . in. . . . the . . . . . . water. No. That's not water. It doesn't begin with "w." S (says letter name) sssss (letter sound). Sea. Fish swim in the sea.

This is the feedback the teacher gave to the student after she finished reading the sentence:

> You did a very good job of using your strategies to read the text accurately. Let's keep on reading and while you are reading think about whether what you are reading makes sense, and does what you are seeing match with what you are reading?—just like you did when you noticed that water could not be the right word because the word on the page began with the letter "s."

In this example, the feedback the teacher gave to the student:

- Provided verification about what she was doing correctly
- Provided feedback on the quality of her work (reading)
- Provided specific information about her reading relative to learning goals
- Scaffolded her learning so that as she continued reading she was oriented to the cues she had worked on in her reading group
- Reinforced a strategy for self-regulation

Notice in this example that the teacher provided praise for the student—"you did a good job." Although praise alone, or praise that draws attention to the student rather than the task, is not effective in improving learning, in this case, the teacher provided praise with specific information about the task. Terms like "good job" by themselves do not give any indication about the nature of the "job" done. Students might well ask, "In what way was it a good job?" or "How will I know next time I do a good job with this kind of task?" However, while Drew's teacher gave her some praise, it was clearly associated with how she was reading and meeting the success criteria (i.e., using the reading strategies she had learned).

Example 4

In a kindergarten classroom, students were learning how to generate questions to gather information. They were studying the sources of their food and were preparing for a field trip to the local market. In preparation, the students came up with a question they would want to investigate on their trip. The teacher discussed each student's question with them and provided feedback. Some examples of questions and feedback are below.

Student Question: Why do people buy meat from the market?

> Teacher Feedback: I wonder if you can answer your question from a visit to the market. Talk to Laquita about what you think you will see at the market, then decide if you can get the information you need to answer your question. Let me know when you are ready to talk about your decision.

Student Question: How does the milk get from a cow to the carton?

> Teacher Feedback: Remember we have been talking about questions that help us decide on the information we will need to find. What information do you think you need to answer your question? Can you find that information at the market? Think about it and I'll be back to check in a minute.

Student Question: There are a lot of different kinds of vegetables in the market.

> Teacher Feedback: Do you remember when we talked about the difference between a question and a statement? Look again at what you have written and think about whether it is a statement or a question. (Child responds.) Why do you think it is a statement and not a question? (Child responds.) I agree, now see if you can turn your statement into a question.

What were the features of the teacher's oral feedback?

- It was directly related to the learning goal.
- It scaffolded student learning.
- It supported self-regulation.
- It was matched to the students' cognitive levels.

In the previous examples, teachers gave feedback either orally or in writing. One of the challenges of providing useful feedback, particularly for middle and high school teachers, is the number of students they have to teach. While providing oral feedback in the context of a lesson is a relatively quick means of supporting learning, we have to be realistic about the amount of written feedback teachers can give to students. One way around this problem is to provide a combination of oral and written feedback, as the following example shows.

Example 5

In an eighth-grade class, students were critically evaluating historical sources related to a specific time period to reach conclusions about why events occurred and were supporting their conclusions with the appropriate evidence. For a specific writing task, students were given the success criterion "all your conclusions should be backed with evidence." After reviewing all the students' work, the teacher gave the following feedback to the class:

> Remember, the success criterion for this task was that all your conclusions should be backed by evidence. I've used a check mark to indicate the statements that are backed by evidence. Now, you each need to find the statements that are not supported by evidence and provide it.

The teacher used the check marks to quickly identify where students had used evidence and was able to give them oral directions for using the marks to improve their work. This feedback strategy was effective in directing students how to improve their work and cut down the amount of written feedback the teacher produced.

How did this teacher's feedback meet the criteria for effective feedback?

- The feedback was specific and related to the success criterion.
- It verified what was correct.
- It provided information about the qualities of student work.
- It provided cues for subsequent improvement.
- The feedback matched the students' cognitive needs.

Although the teacher marked each student's work according to the quality of his or her conclusions, a word of caution about providing group feedback is in order here. In this example, the teacher provided feedback to the class because she had judged that all students could benefit from the same feedback. What teachers should avoid is providing group feedback when it is relevant to only some members of the group (Nadler, 1979). In such circumstances, an individual student could regard the feedback as not applicable to him, or alternatively regard it as applicable to him when, in reality, it is not. Either way, the purpose of the feedback is diminished and may even have counterproductive consequences.

Example 6

A class of tenth-graders had been examining the way several authors created an atmosphere of tension and suspense in their writing. In particular, they had focused on word choice and phrases to create this effect. The teacher assigned the task of imaginative writing about the experience of someone going into a secret place for the first time. The success criteria were to use words and phrases that heighten the sense of tension and suspense.

In another example of how to use comment markers when providing feedback, the teacher circled words and phrases that were effective in creating the required effects and underlined those that could be improved. Students talked with a partner about why words and phrases met the criteria and used their reflections to improve the ones the teacher underlined.

What was effective about this feedback?

- It was focused on the success criteria.
- It verified what was correct.
- It gave cues for improvement.
- It was neither complex nor vague.

USING THE FEEDBACK

Recall that in Ramaprasad's definition, feedback is only considered feedback when it is *used* to alter the gap. This means that students must use the feedback. If they don't have the opportunity to use the feedback to improve learning, then the feedback is not formative. So when planning for formative assessment, teachers must also make plans for when they are going to provide feedback, and also when they are going to give the students time to use the feedback and apply the comments to their work. Sometimes the use of feedback will be immediate. At other times, feedback will be provided in the next lesson after the teacher has had time to review the students' responses. The important point here is that if feedback is to be formative to learning, it must meet the criteria for effective feedback provided earlier in the chapter, and it must lead to new learning.

WHAT ABOUT GRADES?

Stated bluntly, giving students a grade is not formative feedback. Why? The purpose of formative feedback is to improve learning while that learning is occurring or evolving. Grades operate as summative judgments by providing an evaluation of learning. At the very minimum, it is unfair to grade learners *while* they are in the process of learning. Grades can be characterized as outcome feedback, which only provides information relative to the state of achievement and offers the least guidance about how to self-regulate (Butler & Winne, 1995). Therefore, if teachers need to give grades, these should be given at the end of a period of learning as an evaluation of what has been learned.

Another reason why grades are not part of formative feedback is because providing a grade does not meet any of the criteria for effective feedback. In fact, grades meet many of the criteria that have negative effects on learning, for example, comparisons between and among students, vague feedback, not specific to a learning goal, and with no indication of how to improve. Sadler (1989) proposes that grades "may actually be counterproductive for formative assessment" (p. 121). He suggests that while a grade on a piece of work might mean something to a teacher in terms of the quality of the work, the meaning is almost always "too deeply coded" for a student to translate into action. He argues that grades are "a one-way cipher for students" because they do not lead to action to close the feedback loop.

In a classic study of grades and student performance, Butler (1987) showed that grades alone or comments along with grades did not increase performance. Many teachers try to make grades motivating, for example, by offering extra credit; but even in cases where grades are motivating, they tend to increase students' ego involvement in learning rather than their task involvement, which as we learned in Chapter 4 is a less than effective way to promote learning. Equally, grades can be de-motivating. Imagine the impact on motivation for a student who tries really hard but rarely gets a good grade. However, it is important to remember that the kind of feedback we have examined in this chapter can significantly improve learning, which is the goal of formative assessment. We need to make sure that students are provided with information that supports their learning and their achievement, and there is little evidence to show that grades do this.

It's also important to recognize that, such is the culture of grades in the United States, many teachers may feel guilty when not giving grades, or even feel that they are not doing their job properly. This feeling is exacerbated when school or district policy directs how many grades need to be awarded per grading period—or worse, where teachers are directed to grade everything a student produces. A school feedback policy can help mitigate these feelings. With a clear policy that feedback will be provided to students during the course of their learning, and grades after a period of learning to evaluate the state of that learning, teachers (and parents) will have a clear understanding about the purpose of feedback and the purpose of grades and will know what to expect when.

STUDENT FEEDBACK

Increasingly, with calls for students to "learn how to learn," or develop lifelong learning skills, researchers and practitioners are recognizing the need for student involvement in assessment through peer and self-assessment. As students engage in these practices, they develop the skills that are emphasized in a range of educational reform proposals (Davis, Kumtepe, & Ayendiz, 2007). For example, in peer and self-assessment, students take more responsibility for their learning, become more self-directed, and engage in collaborative processes. In the following sections, we will focus on feedback that comes from peer assessment, and feedback that students generate through monitoring and evaluating their own learning.

PEER FEEDBACK

Teachers are not the only people in the classroom who can give feedback—peers are also sources of feedback for learning. Peer feedback has a number of advantages, both for those students providing the feedback as well as those receiving it. It involves thinking about learning and can deepen students' understanding of their own learning. As Dylan Wiliam states, "research shows that the people providing the feedback benefit just as much as the recipient, because they are forced to internalize the learning intentions and success criteria in the context of someone else's work, which is less emotionally charged than one's own" (2006, p. 6). As we have noted in previous chapters, the feedback students provide to each other can also be a formative assessment for teachers. What students say or write about each other's work can show how well they understand the learning goals and success criteria, and the depth of their thinking about the task at hand.

To provide feedback, peers need to assess the status of an individual or a group classmates' learning against the same success criteria they use to check their own learning. For example, peers may exchange drafts of a speech that has the success criteria:

- Introduce your topic in a way that engages your audience.
- Make an impact on your audience with your ending.

Once the peers have considered the extent to which the criteria have been met or not met, they can provide constructive feedback about how their classmate could improve his or her speech:

> Starting your speech with a question was a good way of getting your audience's attention. I think you could make a bigger impact at the end of your speech if you go back to your question and finish with a sentence that shows how you answered the question.

Similarly, in a situation where students are working in groups to solve a math problem assigned by the teacher, "explain why $(2 \times 6) + (3 \times 6) = 5 \times 6$, and generalizes to $(2 \times n) + (3 \times n) = 5 \times n$," each group can present their explanations and receive feedback from their peers about their use of diagrams, materials, or numbers to come up with their solutions.

Peers can also review and provide feedback on the improvements students have made as a result of teacher feedback. For instance, in Example 6, peers could review the teacher feedback provided on the words and phrases to create suspense and tension, and then give their peers feedback about the improvements they have made. This feedback, in turn, could also lead to further improvements. Similarly, teachers could review the improvements made as a result of peer feedback.

Students need to be taught to give feedback to their peers and this can begin in the early grades. Structuring conversations among students with sentence starters, such as "I didn't understand when . . ." or "you made me think about . . ." or "it was really clear when you said . . ." can help students get started with providing feedback. Later on, students can be encouraged to identify two things they thought were successful about their peers' work and one thing they thought could be improved. From these beginnings, teachers could assist the students to develop feedback further, providing structured time and protocols during the lesson. For example, one student presents their work to another student (one is silent while the other listens). Next, the presenter asks a question to focus the peer's feedback. The peer providing the feedback asks clarifying questions to make sure he or she understands what is being asked. Then the feedback provider takes time to think about the feedback he or she will offer. Finally, the feedback is offered and the recipient is able to ask clarifying questions.

Clearly, the provision of peer feedback needs to take place in a classroom culture that encourages students to be collaborative, and where each student feels safe, both in providing and receiving feedback. Being able to offer constructive advice to a peer about learning is a skill that needs to be taught. In the next chapter, we'll look at the kind of classroom culture that supports both teacher and peer feedback as well as how teachers can help students develop feedback skills. However, there is one other form of feedback that we need to address and that is the feedback that learners provide for themselves.

FEEDBACK FROM SELF-ASSESSMENT

Bangert-Drowns et al. (1991) distinguished between two sources of feedback—externally provided feedback and feedback that students generate internally by monitoring and assessing their own learning. The skills of monitoring and assessing one's own learning are essential to self-regulation, which as we noted earlier in this chapter is a hallmark of an effective learner.

One part of self-regulation involves metacognition, or thinking about thinking (Paris & Winograd, 2003). As students self-assess, they are monitoring their own learning and appraising its status relative to goals. Another part of self-regulation involves developing a repertoire of strategies for learning, along with the knowledge of when and where to use them. Knowing when and where to use the strategies effectively is also a metacognitive activity. Students need to develop three types of knowledge about the strategy:

1. Declarative knowledge (what the strategy is)

2. Procedural knowledge (how the strategy operates)

3. Conditional knowledge (when and why a strategy should be applied) (Paris, Lipson, & Wixson, 1983)

If students have this type of knowledge, they are better able to apply the appropriate strategy for a particular learning task and also to make decisions about changing the strategy when they find it is not working. So there are two main aspects of self-assessment which both support self-regulated learning: monitoring one's own learning and deciding on the appropriate strategy to make progress.

What we want students to be able to do during metacognitive activity is to engage in an internal conversation led by a series of questions. The internal questions students ask will differ according to the domain of learning. For example, in the domain of mathematics, Mevarech and Kramarski (1997) showed how students can use four categories of metacognitive questioning to monitor their own learning and select learning strategies while solving a problem:

- Comprehend the problem (e.g., What is the problem all about?).
- Construct connections between previous and new knowledge (e.g., What are the similarities and differences between the problem at hand and the problems you have solved in the past? Why?).
- Use appropriate strategies for solving the problem (e.g., What are the strategies/tactics/principles appropriate for solving the problem and why?).
- Reflect on the processes and the solution (e.g., What did I do wrong here? Does the solution make sense?).

The responses students make to the questions generate their internal feedback. If the student's response to the question "What is this problem all about?" is "I don't know," then he needs to apply a strategy to discover the nature of the problem. If the student's response to the question "What are the strategies/tactics/principles appropriate for solving the problem?" is "Not this one, it is not working," he can seek help or adopt another problem-solving strategy. Using the categories of metacognitive questioning, the student engages in processes that assess "states of progress relative to goals and generates feedback that can guide further action" (Butler & Winne, 1995, p. 259).

In Example 3, we can see that the student is engaged in metacognitive activity during reading because she self-corrects. As she is monitoring her reading, one of the internal questions she asks is "Does what I read match with what I see?" While she is reading, she realizes when she reads the word "water" it does not match what she sees on the page, the word "sea." At this point she uses a grapho-phonic strategy she has learned to make an adjustment and she rereads the word.

In a third-grade classroom at Para Los Niños school in Los Angeles, while learning about the structure of state government, a student asked herself if she was understanding the structure of government and responded, "No, not very well." This self-assessment prompted her to try to relate the structure of government to the levels of leadership she was familiar with in the school. She drew pictures of the principal, the vice-principal, and the teacher and linked them to the role of the governor, senators, and representatives. When she had completed her representation, she discussed it with the teacher who then helped her make sense of the roles and responsibilities of each. Her internal questioning led her to a point where she needed to take some action—essentially, she took steps to scaffold her own learning.

To support self-assessment, teachers must help students to develop their internal voice. From simple beginnings such as asking questions like "Do you think that your response showed your understanding of . . . ? If yes, why do you think this? If not, why do you think you did not show you understood X?" "What strategy could you use to help you understand?" Students can learn to ask their own questions. Eventually, they will become more independent and recognize when they do not understand, when they need to do something about it, and what they can do to improve.

Three additional ways to support student self-assessment are (1) the use of red, yellow, and green cups described in Chapter 5; (2) asking students write comments on sticky notes at the end of a lesson; and (3) a self-assessment log.

In the use of color-coded cups, students are asked to indicate, as a result of self-assessment, their current level of understanding of the lesson content. Asking students to write on sticky notes at the end of the lesson one thing they are confident they learned in the lesson, one thing they need help with, and one thing that really interested them, and then post on a chart as they exit the classroom prompts students to reflect on their learning. In addition to the benefits of self-assessment, the teacher can quickly review the comments and use the comments about things students are struggling with to plan the next lesson.

A third way for teachers to support self-assessment is to scaffold students' reflections on their own learning. For example, Sharon Pernisi gave her students a self-assessment log to complete at the end of the lesson on graphing coordinates we saw in Chapter 5. The log asked the students to rate their level of understanding in relation to the success criteria of the lesson and to indicate what they needed to spend more time on. In Figure 6.2, we can see how one of her students completed the log. As well as helping the students reflect on their own learning, indicate their status relative to learning goals, and make decisions about what they need more work on, their self-assessment also gives Sharon feedback for making instructional plans.

Figure 6.2 Student Self-Assessment Related to Success Criteria

Think about your learning…

Circle the number that you feel best matches your level of success with each item.

I can talk and write about plotting points using correct vocabulary.

Not at all   Absolutely
1   ②   3   4   5

I can plot points in all four quadrants.

Not at all   Absolutely
1   2   3   ④   5

I can create a rule for ordered pairs (*x,y*) for quadrants I,II,III, and IV.

Not at all   Absolutely
1   ②   3   4   5

After this lesson, I feel like I need more time learning

graphing

_____

_____

_____

_____

In another example of a teacher scaffolding student self-assessment, a class of seventh-grade students were working in small groups with the learning goal of developing ideas for a dance composition from some poetry they had read. At the end of their group session, they completed the following group log to reflect on their learning:

- What was successful about your learning today?
- What difficulties or problems did you encounter in your learning?
- How did you manage those difficulties? Were you successful? If not, what plans do you have for dealing with them in the next lesson? Whom do you need help from?

In addition to providing a structure for students to assess their learning, once again, the teacher can use this information to help guide how she works with the students to move forward to meet the learning goal. In this instance, the teacher and her students are both sharing the responsibility for learning.

The three sources of feedback for learning we have examined in this chapter—teacher, peer, and self—are essential components of effective learning. They should be part of the fabric of teaching and learning in a classroom, all operating together to promote learning on the part of all students. In the next chapter, we will explore how teachers can develop skills in providing effective feedback and in supporting students to engage in peer and self-assessment.

SUMMING UP

- In the classroom, feedback can be generated by teachers, peers, and by learners themselves.
- No matter the source of the feedback (teacher, peer, self), the feedback should help answer three questions:
  o Where am I going?
  o Where am I now?
  o Where to next?
- Not all kinds of feedback have positive consequences. Feedback should have the features that research shows lead to improved learning.
- Teachers can assist students to develop the skills of peer assessment.
- Teachers can support students to develop internal questions to guide their self-assessment.

REFLECTION QUESTIONS

1. What kind of feedback do you provide to your students? Does it meet the criteria for effective feedback outlined in this chapter?

2. How often do you engage students in peer assessment to provide feedback to their classmates?

3. What opportunities do you provide for students to be involved in self-assessment? Is this something you could improve?

4. What have you read about in this chapter that you would like to work on?

Implementing Formative Assessment

What Do Teachers Need to Know and Be Able to Do?

This chapter focuses on what teachers need to know and be able to do to successfully implement the process of formative assessment in their classrooms. Here we are going consider ways that teachers can develop the knowledge and skills needed to become effective users of formative assessment with their students. First, we will consider the kind of classroom culture that enables formative assessment practices to flourish. Then, we will turn to the classroom management skills teachers need to build this culture. Finally, we will look specifically at the range of knowledge and skills that are associated with effective formative assessment and how teachers can develop them.

CREATING THE CLASSROOM CULTURE

In previous chapters, we have seen that feedback to improve teaching and learning is central to formative assessment. We have also seen that feedback can come from teachers, peers, and the learners themselves. Feedback to improve learning involves acknowledging successes toward meeting the learning goal and suggesting ways in which the gap between current learning status and the goal can be closed. For feedback to be effective, students must value it as a means to improve learning, no matter what the source. Feedback will only be valued if the culture established by the teacher is conducive to giving and receiving feedback. Lorrie Shepard helps us understand what such a classroom culture would be when she poses the question, "Could we create a learning culture where students and teachers would have a shared expectation that finding out what makes sense and what doesn't is a joint and worthwhile project, essential to taking the next steps in learning?" (Shepard, 2000, p. 10). In this vein, she quotes Philippe Perrenoud (1991) who argued that "every teacher who wants to practice formative assessment must reconstruct the teaching contract so as to counteract the habits acquired by his pupils" (p. 92).

What does reconstructing the teaching contract entail? First, it means that power in the classroom is not held solely by the teachers, but it is distributed so that teachers and students work together to share responsibility for learning. Second, it means that the classroom has to be a "safe" place. Students must be able to ask for help, regard errors as sources of new learning, and admit difficulties or problems in learning without fearing that these actions will diminish them in the eyes of their teachers or their peers. Instead, they need to know that such behaviors are desirable and are characteristic of effective learners. Finally, it means that the relationships in the classroom must be supportive and collaborative, characterized by mutual trust among teachers and students. In short, reconstructing the teaching contract means reconstructing the learning contract as well.

Classroom teachers are responsible for creating the classroom culture that manifests these elements of the teaching and learning contract. To do this, teachers must establish normative values, standards, and practices in the classroom that support distributed power, feelings of safety, and trusting, collaborative relationships. For example, establishing the classroom norms of listening respectfully to each other, responding positively and constructively, and appreciating the different skill levels among peers will enable all students to feel safe in the learning environment, and to learn with and from each other. This also requires teachers to model the norms of the classroom in their own behavior. As Sizer and Sizer (1999) remind us, the students "watch us all the time. They listen to us sometimes. They learn from all that watching and listening" (p. xvii).

Also, classroom routines and practices must reflect the reality that power does not solely reside with teachers, but it is also shared with students. Interactions with students that focus on the nature of their learning, and the provision of constructive feedback with opportunities for students to use it, can create the expectation that learning is the responsibility of both teachers and students. Frequent opportunities built into lessons for students to be involved in peer and self-assessment also enable students to share the responsibility for learning.

Regardless of the aspects of formative assessment teachers are trying to implement, they will not get very far without a classroom culture that is conducive to giving and receiving feedback. The classroom culture is of paramount importance in the effective use of formative assessment, and teachers must have the necessary skills and attitudes to create one in which teacher and peer feedback and student self-assessment are central to how teachers and students do business.

CLASSROOM MANAGEMENT

It will be evident from the previous section that effective classroom management skills are essential. Walking into a classroom where formative assessment is well implemented, you would expect to see students interacting with each other to give feedback, teachers interacting with groups or individuals to scaffold instruction using feedback based on assessment evidence, and students discussing their task, or asking for help, or seeking out additional information.

In short, you would expect to see a dynamic and interactive classroom. While you will also likely see teachers lecturing to the class, if that is the most appropriate strategy to promote learning in a particular context, for the most part, the traditional forms of "stand and deliver" teaching will not be so evident. So teachers need to have the classroom management skills that permit interaction between them and their students and among students on an ongoing basis. The expectations established by the "classroom contract" provide the framework for managing the classroom. In addition, teachers need to have the skills to organize the learning environment so that resources students need are available and accessible, to engage students in worthwhile learning, and to be flexible in responding to students' needs through structuring differentiated learning groups or learning tasks.

Let's now turn to the knowledge and skills needed for the effective use of formative assessment.

TEACHER KNOWLEDGE

You will see from Figure 7.1 that five components of teacher knowledge are important for the effective use of formative assessment:

1. Content knowledge

2. Knowledge of metacognition

3. Pedagogical content knowledge

4. Knowledge of students' prior learning

5. Assessment knowledge

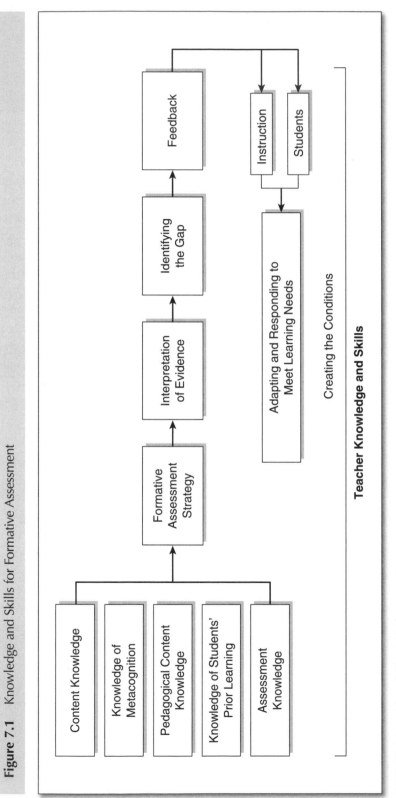

Figure 7.1 Knowledge and Skills for Formative Assessment

SOURCE: Adapted from Bailey & Heritage, 2008.

CONTENT KNOWLEDGE

Effective formative assessment requires teachers to have the necessary depth of content knowledge to answer three essential questions:

- Where are my students going?
- Where are they now?
- Where to next?

Answering these questions requires teachers to be able to define learning goals and success criteria, interpret student responses in terms of what they mean about the status of learning, and make judgments about the next steps students need to take to progress. All of these requirements are dependent on the depth of the teachers' content knowledge: the concepts, knowledge and skills students need to learn, the precursors necessary for acquiring them, what a successful performance in each looks like, and what comes next in learning so that students are consistently building competence in the domain.

To illustrate the knowledge needed for effective formative assessment, we are going to return to Sharon Pernisi's lesson plan we first saw in Chapter 5, which was focused on developing students' understanding of the coordinate plane.

Figure 7.2 Sharon's Success Criteria and Formative Assessment Strategies

Start of Lesson	Middle of Lesson	End of Lesson
Vocabulary check: Whip Around What comes to mind when you think of coordinate graphing? Look for target vocabulary: Origin, x-axis, y-axis, coordinates, quadrant	Large group (SC2): Students walk coordinates and label each location on large floor graph. Describe process verbally using vocabulary (SC1). Plot and label points in four quadrants individually—"Design Robertsville" (SC1, 2).	Cooperative groups (SC3): Generalize quadrant location for set of coordinates verbally and in writing. Chart to create rules for each quadrant and gallery walk (SC3). Reflection: Self-assessment of SC.

Sharon's knowledge of mathematical content enabled her to define conceptual learning goals and provide explicit criteria to her students of what a good performance in acquiring the concepts looks like. Her knowledge of the domain and of how students learn these concepts also enabled her to identify possible misconceptions that could arise during the lesson.

Developing Content Knowledge

If you were to ask Sharon how she developed her content knowledge, she would say that it is through professional learning. She takes advantage of math professional development opportunities in her district, and she reads professional journals about mathematics. She would also tell you that the best professional learning she has is through working with her colleagues. Sharon and her colleagues develop learning progressions for the development of specific concepts and skills. In doing this, they have rich conversations about mathematics content, about what the development of competence looks like, and about the best ways to help students learn. Once they have taught the lessons related to a particular part of the progression, they take time to review the progression and make any adjustments they think are needed in light of experience.

Granted, the process of developing progressions takes time, but Sharon and her colleagues regard this process as essential for deepening their knowledge, and for effective formative assessment practice. Chapter 4 provided some ideas about developing progressions. It is important to realize that all the progressions teachers need do not have to be developed at once. After all, Rome was not built in a day! Picking an area that a group of teachers feel strong in, and practicing developing and reviewing progressions, is a good place to start. Examining research, standards, and curricular materials will help teachers deepen their knowledge, and discussing with colleagues how to take what they have learned and create a learning progression will deepen knowledge even more.

Working with colleagues to decide on how to frame the learning goals for a chunk of the progression, and thinking about what a good performance will look like (success criteria), is also a way to develop and deepen content knowledge. While it may be impractical to do this for every lesson, taking advantage of colleagues' content knowledge is important to do as much as is possible.

In addition to planning ahead of the lesson, it's also a good idea to review the learning goals and success criteria after the lesson to decide if these led to the expected learning based on the progression. Reviewing them with colleagues would also provide another rich opportunity for thinking about the progression.

Before you think teachers can't do that or they don't have the time, remember what is described above is what actual teachers are doing. They make time for professional learning and for collaborating with colleagues because they regard it as essential to being an effective teacher. They also don't expect to do everything at once. Over time, they are creating learning progressions that guide their teaching, and they are developing lessons with clear learning goals and success criteria that match the progression. During this process, they are developing deep content knowledge, the kind of knowledge they know they need to implement formative assessment in their classrooms.

KNOWLEDGE ABOUT METACOGNITION

Because student metacognition is an important component of formative assessment, teachers need to understand what student metacognition entails. Remember from Chapter 6 that effective learners are self-regulated. Students who are self-regulated learners take responsibility for their own learning, they monitor how their learning is progressing, and when they recognize they are not learning they have the strategies to do something about it. This means they engage in metacognitive activity: They are consciously thinking about their learning.

Teachers need to know that to increase their metacognitive abilities, students must be aware of and use three types of strategy knowledge: declarative, what the strategy is; procedural, how the strategy operates; and conditional, when and why a strategy should be applied.

Another dimension of metacognition is motivation. Teacher knowledge about how the classroom culture, the learning activity, and assessment impact motivation is a significant factor in how learning and assessment is organized. In Chapter 4, for example, we learned about the importance of a learning orientation rather than a performance orientation and how each of these affects motivation. Rick Stiggins (2001) describes motivation as the "engine" that drives teaching and learning. An understanding of factors influencing motivation and how formative assessment practices can enhance motivation is essential if teachers are going to be skillful users of formative assessment to promote learning.

Developing Knowledge About Metacognition

There is an extensive literature on metacognition, encompassing motivation and self-regulation. Many schools have professional reading groups, and one way to increase knowledge about metacognition is to focus on reading some of this literature. In reading groups, teachers reflect on the texts and discuss how research findings can be applied in classroom practice.

PEDAGOGICAL CONTENT KNOWLEDGE

Teachers need knowledge of how to teach content, the concepts, skills, and knowledge of the domain. They also need knowledge of the processes, for example, reasoning, problem solving, communication, and collaboration involved in knowledge formation. This knowledge also includes a grasp of the typical misconceptions students have in a subject, together with an understanding of the sources of these misconceptions and ways of addressing them. They use this knowledge in formative assessment to adapt instruction to close the gap between the students' current learning status and the goal. As already discussed in earlier chapters, the gap will differ from student to student. So for the effective use of formative assessment evidence, teachers' pedagogical content knowledge must include multiple, differentiated instructional strategies and knowledge of when and how to use them in the classroom.

Developing Pedagogical Content Knowledge

Building an extensive repertoire of instructional strategies takes time and experience. But there are ways in which teachers can work together to increase their pedagogical content knowledge. Anticipating students' likely responses to tasks can prepare teachers to select the appropriate instructional strategy. If teachers work together to plan learning goals, success criteria, and formative assessment strategies, part of their planning could be to think about the kinds of responses they may get from students. The more inexperienced teachers in the group can benefit from hearing from their more experienced colleagues, and the experienced teachers will surely benefit from reflecting on student learning, and from learning about what their colleagues have seen among their students over a number of years.

Once the likely responses have been identified, then teachers can discuss what would be appropriate instructional strategies for each response level to move learning forward. After the lesson(s) have been taught, teachers can discuss what worked, what didn't, and what needs to be revised. And, in the case where teachers hadn't identified a student response, they could talk about what strategy they used and whether it was effective.

Clearly, it is not practical for teachers to meet to plan every lesson. But building discussion time about pedagogy into regular meetings will help increase everyone's knowledge.

In addition, individual teacher reflection at the end of a lesson about the instructional strategies used to meet learning needs can be valuable. How effective were they? How might they be changed to be more successful? If the individual teacher feels that the strategy was not very successful, but isn't sure how to improve it, then asking a colleague can definitely help.

For effective formative assessment, pedagogical content knowledge is not just confined to the content and processes of learning of a specific subject; it must also include knowledge of ways to teach metacognition. Even if teachers have a solid understanding of what metacognition is, and its role in self-assessment and self-regulation, this does not mean they will necessarily have the pedagogical knowledge to know how to support it in their students. Once again, there is much to be learned from working with colleagues. Even if a group of teachers start from the point of no knowledge, they can talk about strategies, try them out, review their success, and make any changes they think are appropriate.

STUDENTS' PREVIOUS LEARNING

The pedagogical benefits of systematically building new knowledge on previous learning are well established. If teachers are to build on students' previous learning, they will need to know exactly what it is that students are bringing to the table. Knowledge of students' previous learning can include the following:

1. The extent of student knowledge about a particular topic in a specific content area

2. The depth of their understanding of concepts in the content area (for example, the degree to which they can make generalizations through a process of abstraction from a number of discrete examples)

3. The level of their skills specific to the content area (i.e., the capacity or competence to perform a task)

4. The attitudes the students are developing (e.g., the value the students place on the subject, the interest they display, and the students' levels of initiative and self-reliance)

5. The level of their language competence in the domain, for example, the extent and accuracy of vocabulary use, production of grammatical structures, and knowledge of discourse patterns (this is important for all students, but will be especially important for English learners)

Depending on what new learning is intended, the status of previous learning will need to be established so that teachers can make connections for the students between prior and new learning to make the new learning accessible.

Developing Knowledge of Students' Previous Learning

Of course, formative assessment strategies will be essential for finding out what students already know and can do. But before teachers even begin to find out a prior learning, they need to have a clear understanding of the knowledge, skills, concepts, and attitudes they want students to learn. Only then will they be able to ask questions or provide tasks to meaningfully determine students' prior learning. Curriculum analysis to determine the elements of students' prior knowledge that needs to be assessed will be an important first step. For example, if a new skill is to be developed, what prior skill level is needed to be able to access the new learning? The development of learning progressions can help with this kind of analysis. Once teachers are clear about what prior learning students need, they can then decide what strategies to use to see if they have it. And in the event they don't have that knowledge, teachers can go back in the progression and use formative assessment strategies to find out just where student prior learning lies.

Asking students what they know already about particular topics is also a good way to learn about previous learning, though this process will require more than a brainstorm. Questions and discussions will be needed to probe levels of knowledge to ensure that teachers are getting the most accurate information about students' prior learning they can.

ASSESSMENT KNOWLEDGE

To maximize the opportunities for gathering evidence about learning, teachers must know about a range of formative assessment strategies. As we have seen in previous chapters, such strategies can be as diverse as observation, questioning, dialogue, representations, explanations, demonstrations and exit cards. In addition, even though the accepted standards of validity and reliability (see American Educational Research Association, American Psychological Association, & National Council on Measurement in Education, 1999) do not translate seamlessly into the formative assessment context, teachers need to understand that assessment quality is an important concern in formative assessment. As we learned in Chapter 5, knowledge of assessment quality includes an understanding that formative assessment strategies should be aligned with learning goals and success criteria, and that the formative assessment selected is appropriate to purpose—for instance, that the assessment yields an appropriate level of detail to support action. Without quality evidence, teachers may not be able to take the right kind of action that will lead to positive consequences for learning. The purpose of formative assessment is to promote further learning, and a concern in the validity of formative assessment is how effectively learning takes place in subsequent instruction (Stobart, 2006).

The purpose of formative assessment is to provide reliable feedback about learning. But because formative assessment enables teachers to repeatedly sample student performance over time, standard indices of reliability are less central in formative assessment as compared with other kinds (Messick, 1995). However, teachers need to be aware that the evidence from the formative assessment strategies and the inferences they draw from it must be of sufficient quality to enable them to understand where the learner is in relation to the success criteria and the learning goal.

As we learned in Chapter 5, assuring quality in formative assessment depends on the following:

- The formative assessment strategy's alignment with the learning goal and success criteria
- Giving students multiple opportunities to show their learning in a range of different knowledge representations (e.g., explanation, demonstration, representation, discussion)
- Frequent collection of evidence in relation to the learning goal
- Sufficiently detailed information to provide the basis for action
- Assessment strategies that can capture the range of levels of learning among the students[1]

A further aspect of teachers' assessment knowledge concerns the source of evidence. Teachers will need to know that their own assessment strategies of learning are not the only available source of evidence for determining students' current learning status. As we have emphasized throughout this book, students' self-assessment as well as peer assessment play a big part of formative assessment. Teacher knowledge about self- and peer assessment should include understanding of how the evidence from these sources contributes to improving learning and how teacher feedback and student feedback can be effectively woven into the entire process of formative assessment.

Developing Assessment Knowledge

As we have seen in previous sections, teacher collaboration is an effective way to improve knowledge about formative assessment strategies. For example, to make sure they are addressing issues about assessment quality, teachers may work in groups to identify possible strategies to elicit evidence as they plan their learning goals and success criteria, asking questions such as "Is the strategy aligned to the learning goal and success criteria?" and "Am I using enough strategies with a range of knowledge representations to get information that is as accurate as possible?" Then the teachers could implement the strategies and come together in grade-level or department meetings to examine the evidence, this time asking these questions:

- What was valuable about this strategy?
- What kind of evidence did I get?

---

1. Thanks to Joan Herman and Ellen Osmundson for their insights in the criteria for quality formative assessment.

- What range of responses did I get?
- Did it give me the level of detail I needed?
- Did my evidence-based action have beneficial consequences on learning?

Refining strategies based on this kind of evaluation will help teachers increase their skills in selecting the appropriate formative assessment strategy, as of course, will teachers' own individual reflections on the value of the evidence they have generated from formative assessment.

TEACHER SKILLS

You will see from Figure 7.3 that it is not only teacher knowledge that is foundational to effective formative assessment, but teacher skills as well. In fact, the practice of formative assessment is an interplay of knowledge and skills. In this section, we will focus specifically on the following skills:

1. Interpreting evidence

2. Matching instruction to the gap

3. Providing feedback

4. Teaching metacognitive skills

5. Teaching peer assessment

Figure 7.3   Knowledge and Skills for Formative Assessment

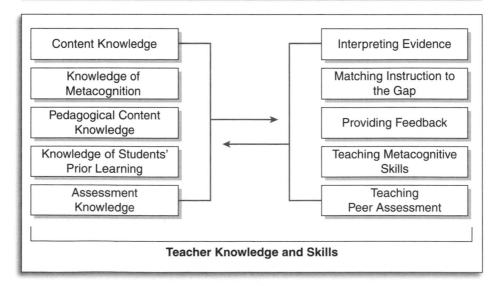

SOURCE: Adapted from Bailey & Heritage, 2008.

INTERPRETING EVIDENCE

Teachers' skills in drawing inferences from formative assessment evidence are pivotal to the effectiveness of formative assessment. No matter what the assessment strategy—observation, dialogue, demonstration, written response—teachers must examine the student response from the perspective of what it shows about their conceptions, misconceptions, skills, and knowledge. This involves a careful analysis of the response in relation to the criteria for success. An analysis of the response leads the teacher to draw inferences with reference to the learning goal. In essence, they need to infer what the "just right gap" is between the current learning and desired goals, identifying students' emerging understanding or skills so that they can build on these by modifying instruction to facilitate growth.

The analysis and interpretation of student responses takes place in different time frames. When evidence arises spontaneously (i.e., teachers haven't planned the strategy before the lesson), teachers will have to make inferences on a moment-by-moment basis. At other times, teachers will be able to review evidence after the lesson—for instance, exit tickets or student work products—when they will have opportunity for closer examination and analysis. In both cases, there is a relationship between content knowledge and interpretive skills. Teachers will need to have the skills of analysis and interpretation. However, teachers' content knowledge provides the backdrop against which the evidence is interpreted. Appropriate inferences about learning are dependent on the breadth and depth of that knowledge, as are the consequences for learning. For example, an inaccurate analysis of students' learning status based on limited or superficial content knowledge may lead to errors in determining what the next learning steps should be, rendering the process of formative assessment ineffective.

Developing Skills in Interpreting Evidence

Just as opportunities for professional learning discussed earlier in the chapter can lead to increases in content knowledge, so can they help teachers in developing analysis and interpretation skills. Working in teacher groups, or faculty, grade-level, or department meetings to analyze student responses—for example, math strategies, written work, and other representations in terms of what it shows about the status of learning relative to desired goals or what misconceptions or gaps in learning are revealed—is an extremely useful way to increase analytic skills, and very likely content knowledge as well. Teachers sharing points from student discussions, describing to colleagues how they interpreted the information, and getting feedback from colleagues is another way to improve analysis skills. Taking opportunities to observe each other in relation to interpretations of evidence from both planned and spontaneous formative assessment that occur in a lesson and then engaging in a debriefing session is also another good way to build skills. Of course, practicing analyzing and interpreting evidence will also increase teachers' skill levels, but only if they have sufficient content knowledge. This means strategies to develop content knowledge must go hand in hand with developing skills in analyzing and interpreting evidence.

PROVIDING FEEDBACK

The analysis of formative assessment evidence will provide the substance for feedback to students. Teachers need the skills to translate the substance into clear and descriptive feedback, matched to the criteria for success that can be used by students to further their learning. As we saw in Chapter 6, this feedback needs to indicate to the students how their response differed from the criteria for success, what they and the teacher need to do to close the gap and how they can do it. Once again, the skills of providing feedback interact with content knowledge, particularly knowledge of what it looks or sounds like when students are meeting the criteria and what it looks or sounds like when they are not.

Developing Skills in Providing Feedback

Teachers need a lot of practice to become effective providers of feedback, and they also need a lot of feedback on their feedback. Asking internal questions as they provide the feedback is one way teachers can develop feedback skill, for example, "Is this feedback clear and understandable? Does it convey to students where they are in relation to success criteria? Will students know what to do as a result of the feedback? Will it lead to improved learning?" If the answer to the questions is not "yes," then some changes need to be made to the feedback.

Sharing feedback with colleagues is also a way to develop skills. Teachers might decide on feedback as their focus for improving formative assessment practices and commit time at grade-level meetings to show feedback they have given to their students, with their colleagues providing comments and suggestions. They may also examine student products where teacher feedback has been used to improve them and discuss if they think the feedback led to solid improvement or not—and if not, what other feedback might have been more useful.

Classroom observation is another way to help each other improve feedback. Watching a colleague give feedback to their students and debriefing after the lesson provides an excellent opportunity for teachers to learn from each other.

We must not forget the students will be an important source of information about feedback. If teachers ask their students about the value of the feedback they gave in relation to the questions they use for their own reflection, they are sure to get insights into how they can improve their feedback skills, especially, if one of the questions for students is "How could this feedback be more useful to you?"

MATCHING INSTRUCTION TO THE GAP

It is axiomatic to formative assessment that if the next instructional steps to close the gap are too hard for the student, frustration will almost certainly result, and if it they are too easy, boredom and disaffection are likely to occur. Therefore, to successfully close the gap, teachers need the skills to translate their interpretations of formative assessment evidence into pedagogical action matched to the learning needs. Remember, the gap will differ among students, so the pedagogical action teachers decide on will need to take this into account. Matching the instruction to the gap cannot be successfully accomplished without allowing for differentiation in classroom instruction. The skills involved in matching instruction to the gap interact with pedagogical content knowledge so that teachers are selecting the appropriate strategy according to students' needs. This means teachers need to decide on the learning experiences that will place appropriate demands on the student, and order them in such a way that each successive element leads the student toward realizing the desired goal.

Teachers' skills in deciding on the appropriate strategy must be complemented by their skills in executing the strategy. Their job is to ensure that the student receives appropriate support in the acquisition of new learning so that the learning is incrementally internalized and, ultimately, becomes part of the student's independent achievement.

Developing Skills in Matching Instruction to the Gap

This is one of the most difficult skills teachers need to learn. There are no shortcuts to developing the skill. Discussing evidence from formative assessment with colleagues and deciding on appropriate next steps is one way to develop the skill. Reflecting on teaching and learning after implementing the pedagogical strategy and asking the question,

"Did this seem like the right match between where the student was and where he needed to go?" is another. Reflecting on student progress and asking, "Did the student make the progress I expected? If not, what would be a more appropriate match between my instruction and her current learning?" is also helpful in deciding if the strategy was the right one. We should also not forget that students are a very good source of information. Asking them if they felt the learning was too hard, too easy, or about right can give teachers good indications of whether they had matched the strategy to the gap.

Finally, being observed by a peer can give teachers valuable information as the whether they have appropriately matched instruction to the gap.

TEACHING PEER ASSESSMENT

Teacher skills also include helping students learn to give constructive feedback to one another that can provide for future growth. From simple beginnings like, "It wasn't clear to me when . . . , "I didn't understand your point about . . . ," and "Your explanation was very clear," student skills in feedback can progress to a detailed analysis of their peers' performance against specific criteria for success

Also, teachers must have the skills to model interactions with students so that they see that they are collaborators with their teacher and peers in developing a shared understanding of their current learning status and what they need to do to move forward.

Developing Skills in Teaching Peer Assessment

Working with colleagues to agree on some sentence starters such as "I'd like to suggest . . . ," "Have you thought about . . .?," "I wasn't clear what you meant when you said . . . ," can be a beginning for developing skills in teaching peer feedback. Teaching the students how to use the sentence starters to provide feedback to their peers, making some notes about what they said in their feedback, and then sharing these with colleagues can help teachers refine the sentence starters or discuss other ways of teaching peer feedback skills.

Other ways of working with teacher colleagues to develop these skills include the following:

- Role playing with other teachers how to give feedback on a piece of student work and then demonstrating this to the students as an exemplar, along with a discussion of what was effective about the feedback

- Observing other classrooms to see how the teacher organizes opportunities for peer feedback. Listening to or reading peer feedback and reflecting on what was effective, or how students might be helped to improve
- Teachers inviting colleagues to observe them and their students when peer feedback is part of the lesson, and debriefing afterward about what was successful, what could improve, and how to help students become more skilled

Even if teachers have all the required knowledge and skills for formative assessment, without the appropriate attitudes toward the role that formative assessment can have in teaching and learning, their knowledge and skills may lie dormant.

TEACHER ATTITUDES

The attitude that formative assessment is integral to instruction and essential to learning is a prerequisite for skillful use of formative assessment. Teachers must view formative assessment and the teaching process as inseparable, recognizing that one cannot happen without the other.

If students are going to be successfully involved in monitoring and assessing their own and their peers' learning, then students need to be regarded by their teachers as partners in learning. To be partners with students in learning, teachers have to invite students into the process, making them active consumers of information, rather than passive recipients. A genuine invitation to partner requires distributed authority in learning, where students are responsible with their teachers for learning. Teachers should ask themselves the question, "Who is doing all the work in this classroom?"; if the answer is "the teacher," something needs to change. Students need to take responsibility for their learning since no one else can learn for them. This does not mean that teachers cede all authority and responsibility to the students. Far from it. Teachers need to remain in charge of learning, while managing teaching and learning to maximize the responsibility students take for their own learning. The answer to the question "Who is doing all the work?" in any classroom should be "The students!"

In the next chapter, we are going to focus on specific structures and practices that can be established within a school to support the development of the knowledge and skills teachers need to successfully implement formative assessment.

SUMMING UP

- Teachers must establish a classroom culture where students feel safe to give and receive feedback for learning.
- A classroom culture where students feel safe is characterized by distributed power, and trusting, collaborative relationships.
- There are five components of teacher knowledge which are important for the effective use of formative assessment: (1) content knowledge; (2) pedagogical content knowledge; (3) knowledge of students' previous learning; (4) knowledge of metacognition; and (5) knowledge of assessment.
- Effective formative assessment requires teachers to have certain skills: (1) interpreting evidence; (2) matching instruction to the gap; (3) providing feedback; (4) supporting metacognitive skills; and (5) teaching peer assessment.
- For most teachers, implementing formative assessment practices will mean some change in how they do business in the classroom; for some teachers, it will require a radical change in practice. A willingness to change, matched with a commitment to taking the time and making the effort to develop new skills and knowledge, will be necessary for effective formative assessment.

REFLECTION QUESTIONS

1. How does the classroom culture you have established compare with the features of a classroom culture described in this chapter? Are there any improvements you could make?

2. How would you rate your level of knowledge and skills for formative assessment against what has been presented in the chapter? What do you feel are your strengths? What are areas you can improve?

3. What are some steps you can take to improve your knowledge or skills? Who can support you?

8 Developing and Deepening Formative Assessment Practice

E. Caroline Wylie
and Margaret Heritage

In Chapter 7, we learned about the knowledge, skills, and attitudes that teachers need to become effective users of formative assessment. We also learned about ways in which teachers can develop this knowledge base, for example, working with colleagues to collaboratively develop learning progressions, anticipating student responses as part of departmental planning sessions, evaluating the quality of feedback, and so on. In this chapter, we are going to focus on specific structures and practices that can be established within a school to help teachers develop and deepen formative assessment in their classroom. We will also address the kind leadership that administrators need to provide, and that teachers should expect to ensure they have the necessary support to engage in the work.

A DAUNTING PROSPECT?

To anyone who has read the preceding chapters, it will be abundantly clear that the effective use of formative assessment requires teachers to orchestrate a wide

AUTHORS' NOTE: Any opinions expressed (in the publication) are those of the author(s) and not necessarily of Educational Testing Service.

range of knowledge and skills simultaneously. This simultaneous orchestration may present a daunting prospect, and both teachers and the administrators who support them may wonder where to start. Should they start with developing skills in feedback, or would they be better to focus on building their content knowledge? Or should they start by making changes to the classroom culture? To help us think about where to start, let's take a moment to consider how athletes train. In many sports, core strength, form, and flexibility are all important attributes. However, an athlete does not focus on "fixing" one area—for example, working solely on flexibility—before moving on to issues of form. Instead, he or she continually works on all these areas together, increasing both strength and flexibility incrementally. Similarly, a teacher does not have to have perfect classroom management before she can begin to think about student metacognition. Indeed, just as incrementally improving core strength may lead to improvements in form, working on supporting students to think more deeply about their own learning, for example, may impact teachers' content and pedagogical content knowledge. What holds true for athletes holds true for teachers. Teachers can engage in professional development for building all their formative assessment muscles incrementally, just as athletes do. It's important to plan for success by taking incremental, small steps that will ultimately lead to giant strides.

A PROFESSIONAL CULTURE FOR CHANGE

Implementing formative assessment means "changing the way a teacher thinks about their teaching and their view of their role as a teacher" (Black, Harrison, Lee, Marshall, & Wiliam, 2003, p. 80). This is a powerful statement, and it is one that rings true with our experiences of working with teachers. Formative assessment practice requires teachers to think differently about the relationship between instruction and assessment, to see feedback as a central mechanism in promoting learning, and to come to regard students as partners in the learning process. Such fundamental shifts in practice take time, commitment, and patience on the part of both teachers and administrators. When embarking on a program of professional development designed to support teachers' use of formative assessment, both administrators and teachers must realize they are in it for the long haul.

Making changes in practice can be scary, and so it is essential that a school culture be established that will support all participants through a change process. First, the leadership in the school has to be committed to formative assessment. Ultimately, formative assessment cannot be a subcontract of individual teachers. Students within a school need to have consistent experiences of being partners in learning, of understanding learning goals and success criteria, and of giving and receiving feedback. Leaders have to provide the vision as well as the time structures to permit teachers to come together to develop their knowledge and skills. They have to support risk taking so that teachers feel they can make mistakes as they try out strategies of formative assessment. Essentially, leaders have to create a culture in which teachers see mistakes as sources of new learning, just as teachers need to create the same culture for their students.

Relationships among teachers and between administrators and teachers have to be characterized by respect and trust. Teachers need to feel they can learn with and from each other. School leaders will also play a big part in establishing the climate for these kinds of relationships and will need to model collaborative relationships with their faculty.

In the next section, we are going to consider how professional development to support teachers can occur within a context of a culture supportive to teacher learning. The recommendations we provide are based on our extensive work in several states to help teachers become skillful users of formative assessment in their classrooms.

PROFESSIONAL DEVELOPMENT TO SUPPORT TEACHERS' USE OF FORMATIVE ASSESSMENT

Consideration of how to support teachers must begin with what we know about effective professional development. Research on professional development, recently summarized by Darling-Hammond, Wei, Andree, Richardson, and Orphanos (2009), indicates that effective professional development should

- be intensive, ongoing, and connected to practice (p. 9).
- focus on student learning and address the teaching of specific curriculum content (p. 10).
- align with school improvement priorities and goals (p. 10).
- build strong working relationships among teachers (p. 11).

School-based professional learning communities (PLCs), where groups of teachers come together on a regular basis to discuss their work, meet all of the research-based professional development criteria. PLCs provide opportunities for teachers to learn in intensive and ongoing ways. They can be focused on student learning, make direct connections to the everyday work of teachers, and support the development of strong working relationships among teachers. In addition, a PLC can be structured to enable teachers to engage in ongoing cycles of learn-practice-reflect-revise, an important process in any professional development program (ETS, 2009; Thompson & Wiliam, 2008, p. 40). PLCs provide opportunities for teachers to come together on a regular basis to learn about formative assessment, with time between meetings for teachers to put that learning into practice. Subsequent meetings, if structured appropriately, allow teachers to share recent practice, reflect on that practice, and solicit feedback from peers. Teachers can then, if needed, revise their implementation plans and continue to practice outside of the meeting time. Providing ongoing learning opportunities followed by time to put learning into practice, followed by more reflection and, if necessary, revision to practice gets at the heart of the "learning" of a PLC. This is a slightly different approach to a PLC than what is often considered. Rick DuFour regards a PLC as an opportunity for teachers, administrators, parents, and students to work together to decide what are best practices, with a focus on results. Then these practices are tested in the classroom and continuously improved (All Things PLC, n.d.). In this approach, the focus is directly on student learning: finding practices that might impact student learning, trying them out, and then collecting data to see if there was the intended impact. In the approach we propose here, we consider the "learning" of the PLC to really be the *teachers'* learning. A PLC focused on formative assessment does not have to search out practices that might impact student learning: There already is a strong body of literature that can support the claim that formative assessment practices, well implemented, will impact student learning. However, knowing what good practice is and doing it on a consistent basis are two different things. Teachers need a process that will support their formative assessment implementation and allow them to refine practices rather than dismissing something early on because it did not have the intended impact: The actual outworking of the practice may need "practice" before it will be effective. As a group of teachers develop and deepen their formative assessment practice, student learning will necessarily be at the forefront since formative assessment is all about moving learning forward.

PLANNING FOR PLCs

We have found initial planning to be very beneficial to the work of the PLC. However, no plans should be set in stone. They can be modified after a few months or after the first year if a review suggests that some changes are needed. Here are some considerations to bear in mind as you make plans for the PLC.

Who Should Participate First?

Three possible options for initial participation in the PLC are (1) a small group of volunteers, (2) a particular grade or subject department, and (3) the entire school. There are pros and cons to each. First, starting with a small group of volunteers allows administrators to capitalize on the group of teachers who are the early adopters, those teachers who are generally eager for a new challenge. A second option is to start with a single grade level or subject area. Some grade levels or subject area teachers might have just started a new initiative, so it might be preferable begin with a different group of teachers who will have time to think about something new, and for whom it makes sense to work together on a particular topic or aspect of practice.

A third option is to engage the whole school from the outset. The advantages of this approach are there cannot be a sense of preferential treatment for some groups or individual teachers, there is no concern about how to eventually involve everyone, and logistical arrangements are often easier when all teachers are involved, for example, organizing early closes or late starts once a month.

How Large Should the Group Be?

We have both worked with groups ranging in size from as few as four teachers to as many as 20 teachers, and depending on the specific focus of the PLC, optimum group size may vary. The earlier concept of the learn-practice-reflect-revise cycle (ETS, 2009; Thompson & Wiliam, 2008) may be helpful when considering this issue. If a significant focus of the PLC meeting time is to be spent by teachers reflecting on current formative assessment implementation efforts, then group size can be critical. If a group is too small (fewer than five teachers), there may not be enough diversity of experience and opinions to promote learning from each other. If it is too large (more than eight or nine teachers), it may become easier for someone to disengage from the group and check out, or conversely, there may not be sufficient time to allow everyone an opportunity to share. Of course, if for some reason the PLC is a larger group, there are a variety of ways to ensure that everyone has a chance to participate by using smaller groups, or even pairs, within the large group to structure discussions.

What Additional Resources Can We Use?

Another important consideration is whether there are additional external resources that can be drawn upon. For example, there may be district or school coaches who could be involved in initial planning conversations. This would allow the coaches to learn alongside the teachers, share a common vocabulary around formative assessment (which we have found is critical for successful PLCs), and then provide additional support. Also, there may be teachers from another school in the state or district who already have had success with formative assessment. These teachers might be able to provide insights into how they found time for teachers to meet together, how they approached the task of deepening understanding about formative assessment, or offer examples of practice that worked well.

When Should Teachers Meet?

Time is a scarce commodity in most schools. In the schools that we have worked with, teachers have met using a variety of schedules: weekly, every other week, and monthly. We have also observed instances of teachers meeting for half days at a time during district professional development days. These meetings tend to happen no more than four times a year, and it becomes difficult to sustain momentum and commitment when meetings are so infrequent (Lyon, Cleland, & Gannon, 2008). There are resources (e.g., DuFour, Eaker, & DuFour, 2005) that provide guidance about how to secure common planning time for teachers, with creative approaches to school scheduling. Once meeting times have been decided, it is essential that the time is preserved so that teachers can engage in the work that is necessary to develop and deepen formative assessment practice.

Earlier in the chapter, we discussed that a culture for change is characterized by respect, collaboration, risk taking, commitment, and reflection. In the next section, we provide some suggestions for how this kind of culture can be created so that teachers feel comfortable sharing their efforts at implementing formative assessment, both their successes and struggles, and giving feedback to, and receiving it from, their colleagues.

Establishing Meeting Expectations

We have found that establishing clear meeting expectations from the outset helps build a culture of respect and trust. Here are some starter suggestions establishing meeting expectations:

- Everyone makes the meetings a high priority and comes on time.
- Everyone pays attention and participates.
- Everyone acknowledges that each participant is a learner.
- Everyone acknowledges that sharing both successes and failures in a safe environment is part of individual learning as well as helps the whole group to learn.

These suggestions can be modified, and other specific norms might emerge as a result of discussion. It may also be valuable to revisit these norms periodically to remind the group about expectations.

Establishing Routines

In addition to meeting expectations, establishing routines help create a culture conducive to changing teachers' practice. Routines are important, and are common in various professions. For example, as noted by Shulman (2005), in medicine, doctors' rounds occur in hospitals across the country. One doctor may present the details of the case and the proposed treatment. Others may ask questions, challenge assumptions, and suggest alternatives. Maintaining this routine means that when a group of doctors arrive at the bedside of a new patient, time does not have to be wasted deciding how to structure the discussion of this next case. Establishing the routine for the formative assessment meetings will similarly be important:

- Does the same person lead the meeting each time or does the leader role rotate?
- If the meeting is primarily a book study, what are the expectations of participants? To have read the chapter before hand, or just to have one person read it and share with the group?
- Will there be protocols for sharing student work or engaging in lesson study to structure that part of the meeting?
- Are there expectations that participants are trying out things in their classrooms? If so, how can participants report at each meeting on what they are learning to share successes and to get advice for struggles?

We recommend that if there is sharing of practice in each meeting, a ground rule should be that everyone has to share something. This approach helps build a sense of commitment and accountability to the group, and it sends a strong message that the group is not just meeting to read an interesting book, design a new unit, or develop one or two strong lessons—the ultimate goal is to change *daily* formative assessment practice.

THE CONTENT OF THE PLCs

The decision makers who determine the content for the PLCs will likely vary by school. It may be the principal, the leadership team, all participants, or a subgroup. There is no single correct way to do it, but it is important to ensure that the thoughtfulness behind any decision is communicated clearly to all those who will be affected. Decisions about the content will also depend on where teachers are in terms of implementation of formative assessment.

The "curriculum" for the year should be thought about early in the schedule of meetings. Planning ahead of time is important, but so is flexibility. The

PLC members need to be open to adjusting the plan as needed so that it continues to meet the needs of the teacher learners.

The previous chapter presented some ideas for how teachers could develop their knowledge and skills in formative assessment. All of these can be a focus for a PLC. In this section, we provide additional suggestions for the PLC "curriculum" that we have found to help develop and deepen formative assessment practice.

Book Study

In Chapter 2, we learned about some of the research that informs formative assessment practice. Reading some of this research and engaging in a book study would be a good starting point for a PLC. For example, the current book could form the content for a series of meetings, as could other books such as those written by Dylan Wiliam or Jim Popham. One person could be assigned the task of coming up with one or two discussion questions for each chapter. This role could rotate chapter by chapter. One important question for each chapter is "How does what I've learned about formative assessment in this chapter impact my daily classroom practice?" Starting in this way helps everyone build a common understanding of formative assessment as well as a common vocabulary, which we have found is an important component of PLCs focused on formative assessment.

Developing Learning Goals and Success Criteria

PLCs would be a good place for teachers to plan learning goals and success criteria. Pairs of teachers could identify upcoming learning goals and then determine the success criteria. Next, they could share them with another pair in the group, receive feedback, and revise. Even though the pairs might not be from the same grade level or content area, we have found that this approach works well. The learning goal and the success criteria should be clear to other adults if they are going to be clear to students. Colleagues across grade levels and disciplines are well able to determine if they are clear or not and provide suggestions for improvement. After teachers have taught the lesson, they could discuss how effective they thought the learning goals and success criteria were and gain feedback from colleagues to revise if necessary. Remember, we saw a good example of this kind of revision in Chapter 4 when Melanie wanted to revise her learning goals after the lesson and Sharon helped her do that successfully.

Improving Questioning Strategies

Paul Black and colleagues suggest that "more effort has to be spent in framing questions that are worth asking: that is questions which explore issues that are critical to the development of students' understanding" (Black et al., 2003, p. 41). Questions like these can help teachers access student thinking and provide the evidence needed to keep learning moving forward. In a PLC, participants could focus on upcoming units and lessons and decide on the important questions that will scaffold learning, how the questions will increase in challenge to develop student thinking, and what kind of thinking will be revealed. These questions could be trialed and revised after discussions about their effectiveness, both as scaffolds for learning and as formative assessment strategies.

Lesson Study

In this approach, teachers work in small groups to plan, teach, observe, and critique "study lessons," following a model developed in Japan. A detailed plan for a single lesson is developed by a small group of teachers, which is then used by one teacher to actually teach the lesson. The other teachers in the group observe the lesson, and then together they discuss it. In light of the discussions, the lesson may be modified and implemented a second time by another teacher in the group. After a second round of discussion, the group will write a report of what they have learned from the process. There are many resources available to support this approach such as those produced by Teachers College on Lesson Study (www.tc.columbia.edu/lessonstudy).

As part of the lesson study process, there may be an overarching goal or research question that the group has decided to focus on, such as "to develop students who are curious about mathematics." However, the focus could also be on an aspect of formative assessment, such as "to use learning goals as a mechanism to convey the focus for a lesson and to assess progress during the lesson." There are existing resources and protocols that can provide a structure for a group to engage in lesson study. If the logistics of organizing a small group of teachers to observe one teacher on a regular basis is too daunting, as an alternative, teachers could agree to use a common lesson plan format—even the process of developing the format could be insightful—and prepare a lesson plan in detail to be shared with the group and discussed. The discussion could center on the degree to which important aspects of formative assessment are represented within the lesson and what improvements might be made.

Sharing Student Work

Examining student work in a systematic way in a PLC provides another approach to structuring discussions and learning about formative assessment. For example, two important elements of the process of formative assessment are eliciting and interpreting evidence of learning. Sharing student work provides a way for a presenting teacher to talk about the evidence that she wished to elicit, to demonstrate what was actually done in terms of the task given to students, and then through student work examples, to talk about how evidence of learning was interpreted. There are online resources available that provide protocols that a group may use as a starting point. For example, the National School Reform Faculty Web site (http://www .nsrfharmony.org/) has many protocols that can be used as part of a Critical Friends Group, as well as multiple protocols to guide the review of student work or common assessment results.

Curriculum Development

For a group that already has some proficiency in formative assessment, focusing on a specific curriculum unit can provide a useful approach. Teachers could first identify the learning goals across the unit, and then identify specific subgoals of the unit. Next, they could develop appropriate and varied ways of eliciting evidence of learning, consider likely student misconceptions or struggles based on previous experiences and knowledge of students, and plan for learning and/or instructional modifications. Similar to lesson study approaches, an important aspect of curriculum development would then be to review implementation and make revisions if needed while the unit is still fresh in everyone's mind.

Involving Students

Teachers can benefit from working together to develop strategies to involve students in the assessment process. Deciding on common ground rules to be observed when providing feedback to peers is an important starting point to create the culture across the school in which it is "safe" to give and receive feedback. Planning templates to scaffold students' provision of feedback to their peers, and sharing successes and challenges in supporting students' peer assessment skills, are also strategies that can be used in a PLC to strengthen practice.

Similarly, sharing strategies to help students self-assess can be a useful PLC focus. These could include developing and trialing questions to assist students to be reflective about where they are relative to the success criteria for a lesson, determining ways in which students can think about what steps to take when they encounter a problem in their learning, and end-of-lesson prompts for students to evaluate their learning and provide feedback about what they need to work on. Also, the lesson study observations afford opportunities to see how colleagues are supporting peer and self-assessment. These observations can be a focus for discussion in the PLCs—what worked in the lesson, what didn't, and what could be improved?

Commercial Professional Development Resources

An alternative approach to developing a "curriculum of study" like the one we have described is for the PLC is to purchase an existing program. It is important to ensure there are sufficient materials to guide one or two years of study of formative assessment. Equally important is to structure the groups so that there is a balance between encouraging teachers to make changes to their practice and reflect on those changes, while still providing ongoing opportunities to consider formative assessment in deeper ways.

As teachers develop and deepen their understanding of formative assessment through the PLC, the focus will naturally shift over time. While a book study might be an excellent way to get started, as teachers develop greater facility with the ideas of formative assessment it is important to channel those ideas into more direct applications to everyday practice, such as reviewing student work or developing curriculum with more embedded formative assessment.

Formative Evaluation of the PLC

At the end of the year, members of the PLC should initiate an honest evaluation of what worked, what did not work, and how the work of the PLC can be improved for the following year (Wylie & Lyon, 2009). This is an opportunity to practice what is preached—the review is formative provided there is an opportunity and willingness to adjust practice in light of results. Administrators might lead the evaluation, but the participating teachers' involvement will be critical. In such an evaluation, it is important to consider what the initial plan for the year actually was, to identify and celebrate what was successful, and to be honest about what was not so successful. The goal is to take what did not work in the first year and to make adjustments in the second year so that barriers can be removed or at least minimized.

One way to consider evaluating the work of the PLC is to discuss the extent to which teachers had opportunities to engage in the learn-practice-reflect-revise cycle (Thompson, 2009), as this is an important process in any professional development efforts. This discussion might result in additional changes for the second year, beyond logistical or support issues.

THE ROLE OF SCHOOL ADMINISTRATORS

We have already raised the importance of leadership for the successful implementation of formative assessment. In this section, we are going to consider 15 factors that administrators need to take into account as they consider supporting formative assessment–focused professional development in their schools.

1. The principal and other administrators need to articulate the importance and value of formative assessment. Developing the knowledge and skills needed for formative assessment will involve teachers in intellectually challenging work, and for many, as we noted earlier, significant changes in practice. Before they embark on this work, teachers need to know the school leadership is convinced of the value of formative assessment to student learning.

2. School leaders need be clear that teachers will have support in this effort. Laying out some specific plans about how that support will be provided, or engaging teachers in a conversation about what kind of support would be needed, are ways the school leaders can signal their support from the outset.

3. Teachers need to know leaders will make finding the time for teachers to engage in PLCs a priority. The National Staff Development Council's (NSCD) report on Professional Learning (Darling-Hammond et al., 2009) indicates that a significant amount of time is essential to develop new knowledge and skills. The NSCD report is clear that one-shot professional development efforts do not work. Moreover, even when professional development programs are sustained over six months to a year, those with between five and 14 hours total contact hours showed no statistically significant impact on student learning. To achieve statistical significance, there needed to be at least 30 hours of total professional development. Considering that most schools operate on a 10-month school year, this means approximately three hours per month at the very minimum need to be devoted to PLCs. So ensuring adequate time, both in terms of the duration of the project or focus, and adequate time on a week-to-week basis, is one of the most important roles administrators can play. From the evaluation of the PLC, other systematic issues may come to light. For example, meetings might have been scheduled at a particular time, but teachers might make clear that it would be easier to meet if each department had common planning periods. Perhaps the idea of early release or early close days to accommodate this schedule was raised during initial planning and rejected as being too difficult. Whatever issues are raised, the administrators' role will be to revaluate decisions and explore ways of making it easier for teachers to meet together, even if it requires challenging old habits.

4. Administrators need to remove existing obstacles that cause teachers to use the time allocated for their PLC for other commitments. For example, depending on who is initially involved (if it is not a schoolwide effort), some participating teachers may also be members of other committees, departments, or involved in other initiatives. Having competing demands may take much of their time, energy, and focus away from the PLC and formative assessment. In this instance, administrators will have to figure out how teachers' time can be freed up so they can fully concentrate on developing formative assessment practices.

5. Where possible, school leaders should make connections to other efforts or initiatives that are already under way to help teachers see the value in developing formative assessment skills rather than the work being seen as just another thing that is being added to their plate. For example, there may be connections to literacy- or mathematics-focused professional development that teachers have already been part of. Engaging some of those core teachers could be a useful way to build support for the new effort. Helping teachers see that they already are incorporating some aspects of formative assessment into their practice may increase enthusiasm for the idea of taking those ideas deeper and further, and help teachers see the new work as an extension of existing work. Furthermore, if some teachers have already experienced success with aspects of formative assessment in their classrooms, they can serve as school-based advocates and positive examples. When responding to skeptics who say "that won't work in our school," there is nothing as powerful as a peer who can talk about what they have done and how they have seen success.

6. School leaders must make strategic decisions about the allocation of resources to support the PLCs. For example, if teachers want to purchase materials for the PLC or need substitute cover to observe each other in class-rooms, funds for this should be available.

7. Leaders should work to establish an atmosphere of risk taking and of learning from mistakes. When teachers are making significant changes to their practice, they need to know they won't receive a poor evaluation when a lesson in which they took a risk goes awry. To learn, students need to feel safe to make mistakes, and teachers must feel safe to do so too.

8. Administrators need to project attitudes of patience and commit-ment. They need to appreciate that changes to practice can be slow, and they need make sure that everyone involved has realistic expectations of what can be accomplished by when.

9. School-based administrators must ensure sufficient communication with district administrators so that they understand what the school is trying to achieve. There may be resources within the district that the school can draw upon or there may be other schools working on similar goals. Sharing school-based successes within the wider district also provides encourage-ment for participating teachers.

10. Administrators need to realize they will also be learners. Formative assessment will likely be new for many administrators, and they need to feel comfortable in the knowledge that they do not have all the answers. Learning with teachers as partners, and ensuring that the teachers have the support they need, send crucial messages to teachers about the importance of their work in their PLC.

11. Administrators need to decide how they want to be learners with the teachers. Should they attend all the meetings, some of the meetings, or part of each meeting? In some cases, teachers might feel less comfortable sharing practice that did not go so well with administrators present. Administrators might consider attending the second part of a PLC meeting; the first half of the meeting would provide time for teachers to reflect on and share practice with the group, and the second half would include a more in-depth study of some aspect of formative assessment.

12. During classroom visits, an administrator should be alert to examples of formative assessment that have been incorporated into the teachers' practice. These should be commented on and encouraged. A principal can even use the elements of the process of formative assessment we first saw in Chapter 2 to structure questions about an observed lesson. When the principal or other administrators observe examples of good practice, they can be shared at other faculty meetings.

13. Administrators should modify formative and summative teacher evaluations to recognize formative assessment practice. For example, the edited book by Martinez-Miller and Cervone (2007) provides in-depth information about how classroom walk-throughs can be used by teachers and administrators. The focus is not on "fixing" what is not working, but on looking for examples of practice that are effective, and building from those.

14. Administrators need to communicate with parents about changes they can expect to see in the school as a result of implementing formative assessment. They must manage parents' expectations so that teachers can focus their efforts on their practice. For example, if schoolwide policies on grading and giving feedback are established, these must be clearly communicated to parents with clear reasons for how this change will benefit learning.

15. Administrators should be sure to recognize progress and to celebrate successes along the way. This leads teachers to feel their efforts are both valued and appreciated.

In this chapter, we extended the ideas presented in Chapter 7 for developing and deepening the knowledge, skills, and attitudes needed to become effective users of formative assessment. We have stressed that for most teachers, implementing formative assessment will require some significant changes in how they teach and how their students learn. We also know that engaging teachers in exploring their role and students' roles in formative assessment can lead to exciting changes that benefit student learning. While the journey to skillful use of formative assessment may be long and bumpy, it is surely a journey worth taking and worth supporting. For the sake of our students, it is a journey we surely must take.

SUMMING UP

- School-based professional learning communities are an effective way to meet the guidelines emerging from research about what is required for effective professional development.
- School administrators play a crucial role to support teachers' learning about, and engagement in, effective formative assessment practices, starting with articulating a vision for formative assessment, connecting it to other initiatives, providing support in meaningful ways, ensuring that the necessary time is protected, and supporting risk taking.
- There are a series of questions that need to be answered to establish PLCs: Who will the participants be? When will they meet? On what will the PLC focus?
- Beyond the initial establishment of PLCs, school leaders play an important role in enabling the PLCs to flourish. Actions around classroom visits, walk-throughs, formative evaluation of the PLCs, and the establishment of broader school policies can all serve to support the ongoing work of teachers in the PLC.
- Engaging district staff in supporting the work in the school is also important. They may be able to bring other resources to the school, to share developing ideas about successful practice with other schools in the district, and connect formative assessment to existing district policies.

REFLECTION QUESTIONS FOR TEACHERS

1. What are the structures already in place to support your engagement in a school-based PLC devoted to formative assessment?

2. What are the barriers that might need to be addressed for the work of PLCs in your school to be successful?

3. What are the resources within the school and/or district on which you could call?

REFLECTION QUESTIONS FOR ADMINISTRATORS

1. If you are considering establishing PLCs focused on formative assessment in your school, whom should you first engage in planning conversations?

2. Do current school schedules and policies allow time for PLCs, or do you need to consider larger changes to facilitate teachers meeting together regularly?

3. Will you begin with volunteers? A particular grade level or department? The whole school?

4. How will the group be organized? Will there be a group leader? Who selects what the focus will be?

References

Allal, L. L., & Lopez, M. (2005). Formative assessment of learning: A review of publications in French. In *Formative assessment: Improving learning in secondary classrooms* (pp. 242–264). Paris: OECD Publishing.

American Educational Research Association, American Psychological Association, & National Council on Measurement in Education. (1999). *Standards for educational and psychological testing.* Washington, DC: American Educational Research Association.

Ames, C. (1992). Classrooms: Goals, structures and student motivation. *Journal of Educational Psychology, 84,* 261–271.

Ames, C., & Archer, J. (1988). Achievement goals in the classroom: Students' learning strategies and motivation processes. *Journal of Educational Psychology, 80,* 260–267.

Assessment Reform Group. (2002). *Testing, motivation, and learning.* Cambridge, UK: Cambridge University Faculty of Education.

Bailey, A., & Heritage, M. (2008). *Formative assessment for literacy, grades K–6: Building reading and academic language skills across the curriculum.* Thousand Oaks, CA: Corwin.

Bandura, A. (1997). *Self-efficacy: The exercise of control.* New York: W. H. Freeman.

Bangert-Drowns, R. L., Kulik, C.-L. C., Kulik, J. A., & Morgan, M. (1991). The instructional effect of feedback in test-like events. *Review of Educational Research, 61,* 213–238.

Baron, R. A. (1993). Criticism (informal negative feedback) as a source of perceived unfairness in organizations: Effects, mechanisms, and countermeasures. In R. Cropanzano (Ed.), *Justice in the workplace: Approaching fairness in human resource management* (pp. 155–170). Hillside, NJ: Lawrence Earlbaum.

Bell, B., & Cowie, B. (2001). The characteristics of formative assessment in science education. *Science Education, 85,* 536–553.

Black, P. (2003, April). *Formative and summative assessment: Can they serve learning together?* Paper presented at AERA, SIG Classroom Assessment Meeting, Chicago.

Black, P., Harrison, C., Lee, C., Marshall, B., & Wiliam, D. (2003). *Assessment for learning: Putting it into practice.* Buckingham, UK: Open University Press.

Black, P., & Wiliam, D. (1998a). Assessment and classroom learning. *Assessment in Education: Principles Policy and Practice, 5,* 7–73.

Black, P., & Wiliam, D. (1998b, October). Inside the black box: Raising standards through classroom assessment. *Phi Delta Kappan, 80,* 139–148.

Bloom, B. S. (1969). Some theoretical issues relating to educational evaluation. In R. W. Tyler (Ed.), *Educational evaluation: New roles, new means: The 63rd year-book of the National Society for the Study of Education* (Part II, pp. 26–50). Chicago: University of Chicago Press.

Boekaerts, M., Pintrich, P. R., & Zeidner, M. (Eds.). (2000). *Handbook of self-regulation.* San Diego, CA: Academic Press.

Butler, D., & Winne, P. (1995). Feedback and self-regulated learning: A theoretical synthesis. *Review of Educational Research, 65,* 245–281.

Butler, R. (1987). Task-involving properties of evaluation: Effects of different feedback conditions on motivational perceptions, interest, and performance. *Journal of Educational Psychology, 79,* 474–482.

Chaiklin, S. (2005). The zone of proximal development in Vygotsky's analysis of learning and instruction. Retrieved December 10, 2006, from http://www .education.miami.edu/blantonw/mainsite/componentsfromclmer/Component5/ ChaiklinTheZoneofProximalDevelopmentInVygotsky.html

Clariana, R. B. (1990). A comparison of answer until correct feedback and knowledge of correct response feedback under two conditions of contextualization. *Journal of Computer-Based Instruction, 17*(4), 125–129.

Clariana, R. B., Wagner, D., & Rohrer-Murphy, L. C. (2000). A connectionist description of feedback timing. *Educational Technology Research and Development, 48,* 5–11.

Clarke, S. (2005). *Formative assessment in the secondary classroom.* London: Hodder Murray.

Corbett, A. T., & Anderson, J. R. (1989). Feedback timing and student control in the LISP intelligent tutoring system. In D. Bierman, J. Brueker, & J. Sandberg (Eds.), *Proceedings of the Fourth International Conference on Artificial Intelligence and Education* (pp. 64–72). Amsterdam, The Netherlands: IOS Press.

Corbett, A. T., & Anderson, J. R. (2001). Locus of feedback control in computer-based tutoring: Impact on learning rate, achievement and attitudes. In *Proceedings of ACMCHI 2001 Conference on Human Factors in Computing Systems* (pp. 245–252). New York: Association for Computing Machinery Press.

Corno, L., & Snow, R. E. (1986). Adapting teaching to individual differences among learners. In M.C. Wittrock (Ed.), *Handbook of research on teaching* (3rd ed., pp. 605–629). New York: Macmillan.

Darling-Hammond, L., Wei, R. C., Andree, A., Richardson, N., & Orphanos, S. (2009, February). *Professional learning in the learning profession: A status report on teacher development in the United States and abroad.* Dallas, TX: National Staff Development Council.

Davis, N. T., Kumtepe, E. G., & Aydeniz, M. (2007). Fostering continuous improvement and learning through peer assessment: Part of an integral model of assessment. *Educational Assessment, 12,* 113–135.

Dihoff, R. E., Brosvic, G. M., & Epstein, M. L. (2003). The role of feedback during academic testing: The delay retention revisited. *The Psychological Record, 53,* 533–548.

DuFour, R., Eaker, R., & DuFour, R. (Eds.). (2005). *On common ground: The power of professional learning communities.* Bloomington, IN: National Educational Service.

Dweck, C. S. (1999). *Self-theories: Their role in motivation, personality and development.* Philadelphia: Psychology Press.

Earl, L. (2003). *Assessment as learning: Using classroom assessment to maximize student learning.* Thousand Oaks, CA: Corwin.

Educational Testing Service. (2009). *TLC Leader Handbook.* Portland, OR: Author.

Gaynor, P. (1981). The effect of feedback delay on retention on computer-based-mathematical material. *Journal of Computer-Based Instruction, 8*(2), 28–34.

Green, J. M. (1998, February). *Constructing the way forward for all students.* A speech delivered at "Innovations for Effective Schools," OECD/New Zealand joint follow-up conference, Christchurch, New Zealand.

Harlen, W. (2006). The role of assessment in developing motivation for learning. In J. Gardner (Ed.), *Assessment and learning* (pp. 61–80). London: Sage.

Harlen, W. (2007). Criteria for evaluating systems for student assessment. *Studies in Educational Evaluation, 33*(1), 15–28.

Hattie, J., & Timperley, H. (2007). The power of feedback. *Review of Educational Research, 77,* 81–112.

Heritage, M. (2007). Formative assessment: What do teachers need to know and do? *Phi Delta Kappan, 89,* 140–145.

Herman, J. L. (2006). Challenges in integrating standards and assessment with student learning. *Measurement: Interdisciplinary Research and Perspectives, 4,* 119–124.

Herman, J., & Heritage, M. (2007, June). *Moving from piecemeal to effective formative assessment practice: Moving pictures on the road to student learning.* Paper presented at the Chief Council of State School Officers Assessment Conference, Nashville, TN.

Hoska, D. M. (1993). Motivating learners through CBI feedback: Developing a positive learner perspective. In V. Dempsey & G. C. Sales (Eds.), *Interactive instruction and feedback* (pp. 105–132). Englewood Cliffs, NJ: Educational Technology Publications.

Kluger, A. N., & DeNisi, A. (1996). The effects of feedback interventions on performance: A historical review, a meta-analysis, and a preliminary feedback intervention theory. *Psychological Bulletin, 119,* 254–284.

Kulhavy, R. W., White, M. T., Topp, B. W., Chan, A. L., & Adams, J. (1985). Feedback complexity and corrective efficiency. *Contemporary Education and Psychology, 10,* 285–291.

Leahy, S., Lyon, C., Thompson, M., & Wiliam, D. (2005). Classroom assessment: Minute-by-minute and day-by-day. *Educational Leadership, 63*(3), 18–24.

Locke, E. A., & Latham, G. P. (1990). *A theory of goal setting & task performance.* Englewood Cliffs, NJ: Prentice Hall.

Lyon, C. J., Cleland, D., & Ganon, M. (2008). Letting go of the reins: Learning about scalability in the context of one district-wide implementation. In E. C. Wylie (Ed.), *Tight but loose: Scaling up teacher professional development in diverse contexts.* (ETS Research Rep. No. RR-08–29). Princeton, NJ: ETS.

Martinez-Miller, P., & Cervone, L. (2007). Breaking through to effective teaching: A walk-through protocol linking student learning and professional practice. Lanham, MD: Rowman & Littlefield.

Mason, B. J., & Bruning, R. (2001). *Providing feedback in computer-based instruction: What the research tells us.* Center for Instructional Innovation, University of Nebraska-Lincoln. Retrieved June 1, 2006, from http://dwb.unl.edu/Edit/MB/MasonBrunning.html

McMillan, J. M. (2007). *Assessment essentials for standards-based education* (2nd ed.). Thousand Oaks, CA: Corwin.

Merriam-Webster's collegiate dictionary (11th ed.). (2007). Springfield, MA: Merriam-Webster.

Mevarech, Z. R., & Kramarski, B. (1997). IMPROVE: A multidimensional method for teaching mathematics in heterogeneous classrooms. *American Educational Research Journal, 34,* 365–395.

Messick, S. (1995). Standards of validity and the validity of standards in performance assessment. *Educational Measurement: Issues and Practice, 14*(4), 5–8.

Nadler, D. (1979). The effects of feedback on task group behavior: A review of the experimental research. *Organizational Behavior & Human Performance, 23,* 309–338.

Narciss, S., & Huth, K. (2004). How to design informative tutoring feedback for multimedia learning. In H. M. Niegemann, D. Leutner, & R. Brunken (Eds.), *Instructional design for multimedia learning* (pp. 181–195). Munster, NY: Waxmann.

National Research Council. (1999). *Improving student learning: A strategic plan for education research and its utilization.* Washington, DC: National Academies Press.

National Research Council. (2000). *How people learn: Brain, mind, experience, and school.* Washington, DC: National Academies Press.

National Research Council. (2001). *Knowing what students know: The science and design of educational assessment.* Committee on the Foundations of Assessment. Pellegrino, J., Chudowsky, N., & Glaser, R. (Eds.), Board on Testing and Assessment, Center for Education, Division of Behavioral and Social Sciences and Education. Washington, DC: National Academies Press.

Organisation for Economic Co-operation and Development, Centre for Educational Research and Innovation (OECD/CERI). (2005). *Formative assessment: Improving learning in secondary classrooms.* Paris: OECD Publishing.

Paris, S. G., Lipson, M. Y., & Wixson, K. K. (1983). Becoming a strategic reader. *Contemporary Educational Psychology, 8,* 293–316.

Paris, S. G., & Winograd, P. (2003). *The role of self-regulated learning in contextual teaching: principles and practices for teacher preparation.* Washington, DC: U.S. Department of Education.

Perrenoud, P. (1991). Towards a pragmatic approach to formative evaluation. In P. Weston (Ed.), *Assessment of pupils' achievement: Motivation and school success* (pp. 77–101). Amsterdam: Swets and Zeitlinger.

Popham, W. J. (2008). *Transformative assessment.* Alexandria, VA: Association for Supervision and Curriculum Development.

Ramaprasad, A. (1983). On the definition of feedback. *Behavioral Science, 28,* 4–13.

Russell, M., & O'Dwyer, L. M. (2009). Diagnosing students' misconceptions in algebra: Results from an experimental pilot study. *Behavior Research Methods, 41,* 414–424.

Sadler, D. R. (1989). Formative assessment and the design of instructional systems. *Instructional Science, 18,* 119–140.

Scarborough, H. S. (2001). Connecting early language and literacy to later reading (dis)abilities: Evidence, theory, and practice. In S. Neuman & D. Dickinson (Eds.), *Handbook for research in early literacy* (pp. 97–110). New York: Guilford Press.

Schunk, D. H. (1995). Self-efficacy and education and instruction. In J. E. Maddux (Ed.), *Self-efficacy, adaptation, and adjustment: Theory, research, and application* (pp. 281–303). New York: Plenum Press.

Scriven, M. (1967). The methodology of evaluation. In R. W. Tyler, R. M. Gagné, & M. Scriven (Eds.), *Perspectives of curriculum evaluation* (pp. 39–83). Chicago: Rand McNally.

Shavelson, R. J., Baxter, G. P., & Pine, J. (1992). Performance assessments: Political rhetoric and measurement reality. *Educational Researcher, 4*(21), 22–27.

Shepard, L. A. (2000). The role of assessment in a learning culture. *Educational Researcher, 29*(7), 4–14.

Shepard, L. A. (2000, April 26). *The role of assessment in a learning culture.* Presidential address presented at the annual meeting of the American Educational Research Association, New Orleans, LA.

Shepard, L. A. (2005). Linking formative assessment to scaffolding. *Educational Leadership, 63*(3), 66–71.

Shepard, L. A., Hammerness, K., Darling-Hammond, L., Rust, F., Snowden, J. B., Gordon, E., et al. (2005). Assessment. In L. Darling-Hammond & J. Bransford (Eds.), *Preparing teachers for a changing world: What teacher should learn and be able to do* (pp. 275–326). Indianapolis, IN: Jossey-Bass.

Shulman, L. (2005, February). *The signature pedagogies of the professions of law, medicine, engineering, and the clergy: Potential lessons for the education of teachers.* Speech delivered at the Math Science Partnerships (MSP) Workshop: "Teacher Education for Effective Teaching and Learning." Hosted by the National Research Council's Center for Education, Irvine, CA.

Shute, V. J. (2008). Focus on formative feedback. *Review of Educational Research, 78,* 153–189.

Sizer, T. R., & Sizer, N. F. (1999). *The students are watching: Schools and the moral contract.* Boston: Beacon Press.

Smith, C., Wiser, M., Anderson, C., & Krajcik, J. (2006). Implications of research on children's learning for standards and assessment: A proposed learning progression for matter and atomic-molecular theory. *Measurement, 14,* 1–98.

Song, S. H., & Keller, J. M. (2001). Effectiveness of motivationally adaptive computer-assisted instruction on the dynamic aspects of motivation. *Educational Technology Research and Development, 49*(2), 5–22.

Stevens, S., Shin, N., Delgado, C., Krajcik, J., & Pellegrino, J. (2007, April). *Using learning progressions to inform curriculum, instruction, and assessment design.* Paper presented at the National Association for Research in Science Teaching, New Orleans, LA.

Stiggins, R. J. (2001). *Student-involved classroom assessment* (3rd ed.). Upper Saddle River, NJ: Prentice Hall.

Stiggins, R. J. (2002). Assessment crisis: The absence of assessment FOR learning. *Phi Delta Kappan, 83,* 758–765.

Stobart, G. (2006). The validity of formative assessment. In J. Gardner (Ed.), *Assessment and learning* (pp. 133–146). London: Sage.

Thompson, M., & Wiliam, D. (2008). Tight but loose: A conceptual framework for scaling up school reforms. In E. C. Wylie (Ed.), *Tight but loose: Scaling up teacher professional development in diverse contexts.* (ETS Research Rep. No. RR-08–29). Princeton, NJ: ETS.

Torrance, H., & Pryor, J. (1998). *Investigating formative assessment.* Buckingham, UK: Open University Press.

Vygotsky, L. S. (1978). *Mind and society: The development of higher mental processes.* Cambridge, MA: Harvard University Press.

White, M. A. (1971). The view from the pupil's desk. In M. Silberman (Ed.), *The experience of schooling* (pp. 337–345). New York: Rinehart and Winston.

Wiliam, D. (2000, May). *Recent developments in educational assessment in England: The integration of formative and summative functions of assessment.* Paper presented at SweMas, Umeå, Sweden.

Wiliam, D. (2006, July). Does assessment hinder learning? Paper presented at ETS Invitational Seminar, Institute of Civil Engineers, London.

Wiliam, D. (2007). Content *then* process: Teacher learning communities in the service of formative assessment. In D. B. Reeves (Ed.), *Ahead of the curve: The power of assessment to transform teaching and learning* (pp. 183–207). Bloomington, IN: Solution Tree.

Wood, D., Bruner, J., & Ross, G. (1976). The role of tutoring in problem solving. *Journal of Child Psychology and Psychiatry, 17,* 89–100.

Wylie, E. C., & Ciofalo, J. F. (2008, September 5). Supporting teachers' use of individual diagnostic items. *Teachers College Record.* Retrieved June 1, 2009, from http://www.tcrecord.org ID Number: 15363.

Wylie, E. C., & Lyon, C. (2009, August 3). What schools and districts need to know to support teachers' use of formative assessment. *Teachers College Record.* Retrieved August 7, 2009, from http://www.tcrecord.org ID Number: 15734.

Zimmerman, B. J. (2000). Attainment of self-regulation: A social cognitive perspective. In M. Boekaerts, P. R. Pintrich, & M. Zeidner (Eds.), *Handbook of self-regulation* (pp. 13–39). San Diego, CA: Academic Press.

Index

CORWIN

A SAGE Company

The Corwin logo—a raven striding across an open book—represents the union of courage and learning. Corwin is committed to improving education for all learners by publishing books and other professional development resources for those serving the field of PreK–12 education. By providing practical, hands-on materials, Corwin continues to carry out the promise of its motto: **"Helping Educators Do Their Work Better."**